Praise for AFT...

"*After Savagery* is a fountain of ... goes beyond and gives full meaning to critiques of 'the West and the rest' and of supporters of Israel's settler-colonial erasure against the Palestinian people. Palestine is a revealer—Dabashi exposes the irredeemable racism behind the posture of universalism adopted by the Global Minority (the so-called West), but he also shows the path toward collective liberation from apartheid and its genocidal consequences. The genocide in Palestine has pushed us toward a critical juncture. Suspended between abyss and hope, we have the choice to preserve what remains of humanity and rebuild Gaza and the rest of Palestine from the ashes of this monstrosity."
—**Francesca Albanese**, United Nations Special Rapporteur on the Occupied Palestinian Territories

"Hamid Dabashi is one of the most brilliant and courageous truth-tellers in our grim and dim times. His powerful analysis and poignant words should inspire all who see the flagrant hypocrisy of the West and seek justice for the wretched of the earth."
—**Dr. Cornel West**, author of *Race Matters*

"Arguing that settler-colonial genocide in Gaza is historically an extension of the Holocaust, which itself was preceded by racial genocidal practices in the colonies, Hamid Dabashi considers solidarity with Palestine as a truly universal liberation that exposes the provinciality of Western philosophy.

If readers evade facing Dabashi's compelling arguments, they can't but enjoy his erudition, his almost-poetic literary style, and admire his resolute moral commitment."

—**Azmi Bishara**, author of
Palestine: Matters of Truth and Justice

"Based on a rich survey of poems, literature, and philosophical tracts, Hamid Dabashi exposes how the genocide in Gaza epitomizes a longer history of racism, Islamophobia, and Orientalism that produced the colonial and postcolonial global order and informed Europe's most known thinkers, who ironically perceived themselves as beacons of humanity. An incisive, disturbing, yet thoroughly convincing essay."

—**Ilan Pappé**, coeditor of *Palestine in a World on Fire*

"*After Savagery* illuminates why the Gaza genocide exposes the definitional barbarity of the project of European modernity, of which Zionism is an integral part. The engine of Dabashi's book is the question of what we owe Palestinians beyond their metaphorical meanings for an anticolonial struggle. Rather than solipsistically instrumentalizing Palestinian suffering for rehabilitating the modern West's presumed moral authority or Jewish innocence as 'exilic,' as so many other authors in the post-Holocaust and post-Gaza genre book business do, *After Savagery* enacts a stunning decolonial move through a poetic meditation on an intersectional imagination that destabilizes modernity's genocidal logic."

—**Atalia Omer**, author of *Days of Awe:
Reimagining Jewishness in Solidarity with Palestinians*

"Hamid Dabashi has written a distinguished philosophical reflection on civilization and its opposite, on violence in thought and action, on the role of the imagination in human life, and on the enduring consequences of colonialism. In his work, Gaza becomes a paradigmatic example of the conceptual denigration and attempted eradication of all those whom Western governments and thinkers define as irremediably 'other.' Dabashi's analysis is truly impressive in its erudition, sympathetic breadth of vision, and passionate engagement."
—**Raymond Geuss**, professor emeritus of philosophy at the University of Cambridge

"With formidable rigor, sophistication, and tenacity, Hamid Dabashi situates Palestine at the heart of a global struggle for liberation from the age of European colonialism. *After Savagery* places the reader on a daring path to build a new world that is fit for the 'total human beings' that we are and aspire to be. Dabashi resolutely and defiantly insists that after savagery must come a committed intellectual and political project of resuscitating our collective humanity."
—**Muhannad Ayyash**, author of *Lordship and Liberation in Palestine-Israel*

AFTER SAVAGERY

GAZA, GENOCIDE, AND THE ILLUSION OF WESTERN CIVILIZATION

HAMID DABASHI

Haymarket Books
Chicago, Illinois

© 2025 Hamid Dabashi

Published in 2025 by
Haymarket Books
P.O. Box 180165
Chicago, IL 60618
www.haymarketbooks.org

ISBN: 979-8-88890-450-3

Distributed to the trade in the US through Consortium Book Sales and Distribution (www.cbsd.com) and internationally through Ingram Publisher Services International (www.ingramcontent.com).

This book was published with the generous support of Lannan Foundation, Wallace Action Fund, and Marguerite Casey Foundation.

Special discounts are available for bulk purchases by organizations and institutions. Please email info@haymarketbooks.org for more information.

Cover photograph and design by Eric Kerl.

Library of Congress Cataloging-in-Publication data is available.

Entered into digital printing August, 2025.

In memoriam
Edward W. Said
(1935–2003)

Rest in peace and power, old friend!

بِسْمِ ٱللَّهِ ٱلرَّحْمَٰنِ ٱلرَّحِيمِ

إِذَا زُلْزِلَتِ ٱلْأَرْضُ زِلْزَالَهَا ١
وَأَخْرَجَتِ ٱلْأَرْضُ أَثْقَالَهَا ٢
وَقَالَ ٱلْإِنسَٰنُ مَا لَهَا ٣
يَوْمَئِذٍ تُحَدِّثُ أَخْبَارَهَا ٤
بِأَنَّ رَبَّكَ أَوْحَىٰ لَهَا ٥
يَوْمَئِذٍ يَصْدُرُ ٱلنَّاسُ أَشْتَاتًا لِّيُرَوْاْ أَعْمَٰلَهُمْ ٦
فَمَن يَعْمَلْ مِثْقَالَ ذَرَّةٍ خَيْرًا يَرَهُ ٧
وَمَن يَعْمَلْ مِثْقَالَ ذَرَّةٍ شَرًّا يَرَهُ ٨

القران الكريم
سورة الزلزلة

In the Name of God, the Merciful, the Compassionate

When the earth is shaken its final shaking,
and when the earth throws out its heavy weights,
and humanity cries: "What is this?"
On that Day the earth will tell its news—
For thy Lord hath inspired it—
On that Day people will proceed in their throngs
to see the consequences of their deeds—
So whoever does an atom's weight of good will see it.
And whoever does an atom's weight of evil will see it.

—Qur'an 99

CONTENTS

	AUTHOR'S NOTE	xi
PREFACE	"Exterminate All the Brutes," Again!	xiii
CHAPTER 1	Palestine Is the World; the World Is Palestine	1
CHAPTER 2	Israel Is "the West"; "the West" Is Israel	31
CHAPTER 3	Poetry After Genocide	59
CHAPTER 4	Philosophy After Savagery	79
CHAPTER 5	The Garrison State Versus the Palestinian Camp	103
CHAPTER 6	Palestine Beyond Borders	133
CONCLUSION	Writing at the Time of a Genocide	153
	ACKNOWLEDGMENTS	175
	NOTES	179
	INDEX	205

AUTHOR'S NOTE

To observe, think through, and write on an unfolding genocide and ethnic cleansing of an entire nation is absolutely imperative and yet deeply precarious. "Shock and awe" has often been invoked as a doctrine describing military assaults. Palestinians are dying in their hundreds and thousands. Israel remains unflinchingly murderous. Governments maintain their genocidal partnership with the settler colony. Gaza has turned into a slaughterhouse. Like millions of other helpless and hopeless human beings around the globe, I kept vigilance. It was dark. It remains dark. So much savagery, so little time to pause.

A goal of the unleashed savagery that has so far resulted in more than 50,000 casualties has been to overwhelm and paralyze the global public witnessing this genocide. I began thinking about writing this book almost immediately after Israel resumed its successive waves of genocidal intent against Palestinians and handed my manuscript to my editor at Haymarket just before March 2025. Around that time, US President Donald Trump hurtled the diabolical idea of expelling all remaining Palestinians who had survived Israel's savagery from Gaza, and turning this part of their tormented homeland into a real estate bonanza. The world was left speechless at the sheer obscenity of the idea. A so-called ceasefire that Trump had facilitated in January 2025, soon after he took office, lasted for about two months, while Israel continued to bomb Syria, Lebanon, and Yemen, before resuming bombing of what is left of Gaza and its inhabitants. Meanwhile, in the US and Europe, those who dare object to this horror are subject to malicious campaigns to frighten and silence them, to rob them of their education and livelihood.

The genocide in Gaza will go down as one of the darkest moments in a history that has lost count of so many such moments around the world. But rarely has the entire gamut of the vicious illusion that calls itself "the West" been so top-to-toe exposed for what has defined its entire history, from the slaughter of Indigenous people recorded by Bartolomé de las Casas in the sixteenth century to my painful mourning of the Palestinian genocide in the twenty-first century.

Hamid Dabashi
New York
April 2025

PREFACE

"Exterminate All the Brutes," Again!

It was very simple, and at the end of that moving appeal to every altruistic sentiment it blazed at you, luminous and terrifying, like a flash of lightning in a serene sky: "Exterminate all the brutes!"[1]
Joseph Conrad, *Heart of Darkness* (1899)

Behind every terrorist stand dozens of men and women, without whom he could not engage in terrorism. They are all enemy combatants, and their blood shall be on all their heads. Now this also includes the mothers of the martyrs, who send them to hell with flowers and kisses. They should follow their sons, nothing would be more just. They should go, as should the physical homes in which they raised the snakes. Otherwise, more little snakes will be raised there. They have to die and their houses should be demolished so that they cannot bear any more terrorists.[2]

Ayelet Shaked, former Israeli
Minister of Justice (2014)

As I write these words, I have a copy of Sven Lindqvist's terrifying short volume *"Exterminate All the Brutes": One Man's Odyssey into the Heart of Darkness and the Origins of European Genocide* (1992) on my desk. Lindqvist takes his cue from Joseph Conrad's classic novel *Heart of Darkness* (1899) and carries its genocidal implications deep into African and global history. I keep returning to this book, pleading with Lindqvist, as it were, to hold my mind steady as I write—for I am deeply afraid. I am a distant witness to a genocide. I am aghast and horrified by the sheer savagery of Israelis mercilessly slaughtering tens of thousands of Palestinians without batting an eye—bombing children and their parents, their homes, hospitals, schools, university campuses, refugee camps, mosques, churches, even when they rush to collect food from the few trucks that manage to get through the circle of starvation Israelis have formed around Gaza. There have been days and nights I could not utter or write a word, frantically following the news instead, mostly in Arabic, because most of what I read in English, especially in *The New York Times* and in BBC online news articles, troubles me to my core: the cold-blooded, calculated cruelty of mastering a pernicious prose that seeks to justify this genocide with writing that is inane, tightfisted, derisive, sardonic even.

In *Heart of Darkness*, Kurtz is a European ivory trader who is driven mad by his lust for power over native Africans. Lindqvist was mesmerized by Kurtz's words at the end of the novel: "Exterminate all the brutes!" "What did they mean to Conrad and his contemporaries?" Lindqvist asks in his preface to *"Exterminate All the Brutes."* "Why did Conrad make them stand out as a summary of all the high-flown rhetoric on Europe's responsibilities to the people of other continents?"[3] Lindqvist then cites Hannah Arendt in *The Origins of Totalitarianism* (1951) and her assessment that "imperialism necessitated racism." Toward the end of his preface, Lindqvist engages apologetically with Steven Katz's *The Holocaust in Historical Context* (1994), where the author has contempt for anyone who dares to place the Jewish Holocaust in comparative context with any other genocide Europeans have perpetrated outside Europe. Lindqvist appears to defend his own position—that European colonialism "prepared the ground" for the Holocaust—while maintaining that both approaches "seem equally valid and complementary."

Right now, we have entered a moment of epistemic shift, when the Jewish Holocaust must be brought into the fold of humanity at large. There is another way of thinking about the Jewish Holocaust, a way that marks its unique specificity while also allowing us to bring it into the larger frame of European genocidal reference, thereby connecting it to the erasure of Native people, to the transatlantic slave trade, to the historical colonization of much of the globe. As Aimé Césaire noted decades ago:

> Yes, it would be worthwhile to study clinically, in detail, the steps taken by Hitler and Hitlerism and to reveal to the very distinguished, very humanistic, very Christian bourgeois of the twentieth century that without his being aware of it, he has a Hitler inside him, that Hitler *inhabits* him, that Hitler is his *demon*, that if he rails against him, he is being inconsistent and that, at bottom, what he cannot forgive Hitler for is not the crime in itself, *the crime against man*, it is not *the humiliation of man as such*, it is the crime against the white man, the humiliation of the white man, and the fact that he applied to Europe colonialist procedures which until then had been reserved exclusively for the Arabs of Algeria, the "coolies" of India, and the "niggers" of Africa.[4]

In this liberated sense of understanding the Jewish Holocaust, we can connect it to the successive waves of Palestinian genocide by Zionists, a genocide that has been incremental, increasingly vicious, and that has culminated in the devastation of Gaza. Jews have always been the internal Other of Europe, as the Orient has been its external Other. Witnessing this savagery in Gaza, we can clearly link the Jewish Holocaust to the Palestinian genocide and see genocidal Zionism as the logical colonial extension of European fascism.

To Witness

This war is a war that is not only between Israel and Hamas. It's a war that is intended, really, truly, to save Western civilization, to save the values of Western civilization.[5]

Israeli President **Isaac Herzog**
(December 12, 2023)

As I begin to write this book in the first week of June 2024, Israel has killed more than 37,000 Palestinians. Every single day since October 7, 2023, the world has awakened to more and more terrorizing updates. By the time I finish and send this book to my publisher, that cold and lifeless number and that vicious fact will have arisen to even colder and more lingering terror.[6] I have written much of this book in the early hours of the morning in New York, with the world around me lost in quiet darkness, the bright apparition of my laptop on the edge of a sofa where I sleep for a few hours before waking up and writing again, trembling with fear.

Soon after the killing of Palestinians resumed with full force in late 2023, I published a short essay on the ethical bankruptcy of a statement coauthored by senior European philosopher Jürgen Habermas, which openly disregarded Palestinian lives in the context of this genocide.[7] Back in 2014, I had written a similar piece reflecting on another major European philosopher, Theodor Adorno (1903–1969), who soon after the Jewish Holocaust had said, "To write poetry after Auschwitz is barbaric."[8] I had wondered then about Gaza, and what the systematic, consistent, unrelenting acts of Israeli savagery against Palestinians would mean for "poetry." In both these pieces, and throughout my work, I have been preoccupied with the following question: Are we non-Europeans, Palestinians or otherwise, even human beings in the enduring philosophical traditions of what calls itself "the West"? And what is the prospect of moral and intellectual agency on the part of people at the receiving end of European philosophy and colonialism at one and the same time?[9]

¶

The cruelty of the Israeli army murdering Palestinians with total impunity granted them by the US, the UK, France,

PREFACE

Germany, Canada, and Australia leaves no room for speculation. Palestinians are simply not considered to be human beings, an idea to which Israeli authorities repeatedly refer. "We are fighting human animals," Israeli Defense Minister Yoav Gallant stated on October 9, 2023, "and we are acting accordingly."[10] Day in and day out as the genocide unfolded, I was haunted by this phrase, and I held the entirety of "Western philosophy" accountable for that unfolding terror.

This book is not about a historical past. This book is about a savagery fully evident and present. The first chapter of the Italian philosopher Giorgio Agamben's classic text, *Remnants of Auschwitz: The Witness and the Archive* (1999) is about The Witness. Habitually, Agamben looks at the two Latin words *testis* and *superstes*, the former referring to a third perspective observing two parties in a legal affair and the latter as someone who has been through an event.[11] In Arabic and Persian as well as adjacent languages, the word we use for "witness" is *Shāhid*. The potent example of it is the Palestinian iconic figure of Handala by Naji al-Ali.[12]

Agamben might not take an interest in what the word "witness" in Arabic or Persian or Urdu or Turkish or any language other than Greek and Latin might be. But we ought to take an interest. The word *Shāhid* is akin to the word *Shahīd*, the first means "witness," and the second means "martyr." So "witness" and "martyr" in our languages are very closely related, one who has been a witness, and one who has died for such a testimonial. It is impossible to exaggerate the moral implications of this proximity in our languages.

Like millions of others around the globe, I am at once overwhelmed by the magnitude of terror that genocidal Zionists are capable of perpetrating on innocent and defenseless people. Neither the political nor the poetic urges, nor the secular or sacred citations that might come to mind can come to terms with what is happening in Palestine. Given the depth of this savagery, the vulgarity, and the cruelty we face, we must expose, I thought to myself, directly, the barbaric roots of what has sold itself as "Western Civilization."

Israel is not a country, it is not a homeland, it is not a rooted culture. Israel is a settler colony, a moral depravity created by the West, enabled and empowered by the West. Israel is the most wicked evidence of the West. Israel is every atrocity ever committed around the world in Asia, Africa, and Latin America by the West in a nutshell, staged for the whole world to see. Since its very inception, Israel is the summation of the West, materialized and put on a pedestal. This book, therefore, is about making a crucial adjustment in our perception of Israel: It is not just a settler colony that the West supports, but it is "the West" in its very quintessence. It is the highest manifestation of the calamitous ideology of conquest that calls itself "the West," exposing its murderous roots and occasioning the groundwork for the very metaphysics of barbarism that has sold itself to the world as "Western civilization." Today, Gaza and the rest of Palestine is where the false premise of Western moral authority is buried. The world is liberated from that false consciousness.

To Read

Mainstream media outlets wish to start the history of the current genocide on October 7, 2023; Palestinians have a natural tendency to go much deeper into history—and rightly so.[13] However, Gaza since October 7, 2023, must be treated as its own phenomenological context—for moral, political, and epistemological reasons. The period since October 7 requires its own hermeneutic circle; we must bear witness around and through the ruins.

It is impossible to exaggerate the terrorizing fact of the days we are living. The political and military might of the entire "Western" world that thought and sold itself as the crowning achievement of our humanity did nothing and, in fact, aided and abetted the mass murder of tens of thousands of innocent Palestinians. The proudest achievement of "Western civilization," which is "Western philosophy," as it calls itself, the history it has colonized for itself, from Plato and Aristotle to Hegel and Heidegger, were all summed up in the miserable statement by the senior-most European philosopher Jürgen Habermas.[14]

We the people of the world—especially in the Global South but extending to the non-White, immigrant, exilic, and refugee communities in the north—are categorically outside the racist apartheid mind of the "Western" philosophical system. We are the wretched of this earth. That deeply and irretrievably tribal epistemic system that calls itself "the West" is exclusive to white Europeans and does not allow others around the world entry into that system—nor should we wish to enter that system. For that racist epistemic system must be morally, imaginatively, and politically dismantled. We in Asia, Africa, Latin America are a metaphysical menace to "Western philosophy," and we are easily physically eliminated the same way that we are metaphysically denied our existence. The history of European colonialism is the history of the physical elimination of what had already been metaphysically marred and marked as troublesome—thus, the entire course of philosophy to the east of Plato is falsely alienated, Orientalized, exoticized, and dismissed, while the Christian and Jewish disposition of the selfsame philosophy westward is celebrated as "philosophy." This savage European colonialism does physically to the body of the colonized what "Western philosophy" had already done to their soul—defined it as an ontological impossibility.

When the Israeli President Isaac Herzog, of Polish, Russian, and Lithuanian origin, says he is defending "Western civilization," he is absolutely right. The garrison state over which Mr. Herzog presides is the last bastion of the genocidal history of Western civilization, a history that covers the genocide of Native Americans, transatlantic slavery, the German slaughter of the natives in Namibia, and the European Jewish Holocaust. What we face in Gaza is not only the fate of millions of human beings whom, on behalf of its "Western supporters," Israel slaughters at will. We must also grapple with how to read this colossal injustice in a prose and politics that overcomes the monumental propaganda normalizing, justifying, excusing this genocidal urge. We need and we must categorically alter the discourse, beginning with the body and soul of Palestinians.

Israeli genocide in Gaza is the terminal state of genocidal colonialism after a long and languid history around the globe. In his seminal essay, "Settler Colonialism and the Elimination of the Native" (2006), Patrick Wolfe wrote: "The question of genocide is never far from discussions of settler colonialism. Land is life—or, at least, land is necessary for life. Thus contests for land can be—indeed, often are—contests for life."[15] On behalf of its Western *alliance* (*alliance* not *allies*), Israel has intentionally committed crimes against humanity to transform the Palestinian national liberation movement into a "humanitarian crisis." The term "humanitarian crisis" was deliberately designated by US and European media outlets and politicians to avoid calling it for what it is: a genocide.

The connective thread between Israel and the murderous mirage of the West are outlets like *The New York Times* in the US and the BBC in the UK, as representative of the entire landscape of corporate—liberal or reactionary—and state-sponsored media. Rather than telling the truth as it is, these media platforms sustain the status quo: the political and normative supremacy of the dysfunctional American empire and all its subsidiaries, particularly its biggest military investment in Israel as a useful settler colony. The result is not fake news. It is processed news, just like processed food, full of chemicals, additives, preservatives, and artificial coloring.

Due to their investment in liberal imperialist ideology, mainstream media outlets do not like Israeli extremism when it is too enthusiastic in its slaughter of Palestinians. A steady dose of slaughter is preferable, which these outlets can justify as "retaliation" or with the mantra of "Israel must defend itself." They dislike Netanyahu as much as they do Trump. They prefer Biden, Clinton, and Obama as liberal imperialists, and they would prefer to see a similar liberalism in Israel so that they can put Israel on a pedestal as a beacon of democracy. On the surface, it may appear as if their editorial boards care about human suffering in Palestine or that they monitor and note Israeli abuses. But these are all, in fact, feeble and threadbare attempts at damage control, because they know that people around the world are horrified. We have to learn how to read the BBC and *The New York Times* contrapuntally, to practice reverse reading, read them forward and then backward—there and then, we see the dynamics of liberal ideology in the service of the ruling regimes of normative knowledge.

To Comprehend

[Palestinians are] horrible, inhuman animals.[16]
Former Israeli Ambassador to the United Nations
Dan Gillerman (October 27, 2023)

How are we to read and comprehend the unrelenting Israeli slaughter of Palestinians by any means necessary—militarily, diplomatically, financially, through starvation, infanticide, targeting the civilian population, destroying the infrastructure of a civic life, schools, hospitals, museums, refugee camps, UN shelters—all amounting to the most vicious act of genocide documented on a daily basis in the digital age?[17]

I have previously argued and demonstrated in historical detail how the idea of "the West" is a delusional byproduct of the ideology of capitalist modernity on one side and the ravaged earth on the other, with a militant conception of "Islam" as a particularly potent and unfortunate consequence of that binary opposition. Since October 7, 2023, the coded category of "the West" has been staged on the global scene with a soaring savagery scarcely seen since European conquerors slaughtered Native Americans, or since Germans and Belgians murdered Africans, or since the English, the French, the Dutch, or the Portuguese massacred elsewhere.[18]

"The West" reasserts itself as the colonially crafted artifice that it has always been. Massive social uprisings against the racist foundations of the West have exposed its colonial roots and malignant distortion of factual histories. The task at hand is twofold: to reveal the colonial origins of the West, and to dismantle its gaudy claim to moral authority.

The West is the existing political order. Palestine stands for the ravaged earth. What Israel is doing in Palestine is not just what all European colonizers have done in Asia, Africa, and Latin America, but is what the West has done to the globe: massive military savagery for control of the wretched of the earth as disposable labor, bereft of dignity and pride of place. The Europe that gave birth to the Israeli settler colony is a tribe that has falsely universalized its clannish lore into universal philosophical truth. The life of a non-European means nothing in European moral and philosophical systems. We need to start from that mortal fact on the ground and build from there.

For over a century now, Zionism has offered Zionists anything but safety and security. Quite the opposite: Stealing land and turning it into a garrison state for the interests of the West is not exactly offering a haven for anyone living in that settler colony. Israel was created by British colonialism to protect the regional interests of British colonialism. Israel is sustained in power by the US in order to protect the interests of the US in the region and in the world. Israel is integral to

"Western interests," both regionally and globally, because it is the trademark of Western imperialism. The singular significance of Israel for the US and Europe is its military base as a garrison state.

The Metaphysics of Barbarism

There is, therefore, only a single categorical imperative and it is this: Act only in accordance with that maxim through which you can at the same time will that it become a universal law.[19]

Immanuel Kant, *Groundwork of the Metaphysics of Morals* (1785)

Gaza is no longer just a piece of land in the remnants of Palestine. It is the ground zero of our postapocalyptic history. It is our new categorical imperative. The Palestinian is the new *Muselmann*, literally "the Muslim," as Agamben puts it, the Untestifiable, the human animal, as Israeli warlords have said. If we were to redraft Kant's categorical imperative today, it would have to be found under the rubble of Gaza.

We therefore need to go to the moral and philosophical roots of the project of Western savagery (as we have experienced it throughout the ravaged world) and reverse the Kantian proposition of the metaphysics of morals to the metaphysics of barbarism. That metaphysics needs active re-theorization from the ruins of Gaza. The West has tasked itself with a civilizing mission not just as a colonial project but also as a moral and philosophical blueprint. This is perhaps what Adorno meant when he said that to compose poetry after Auschwitz is barbarism. Gaza is today's Auschwitz—for the memory of Auschwitz now belongs to Palestinians. The task at hand is not to compose or decompose poetry. The task at hand is to read the metaphysics of morals at the foundation of "Western civilization" as a metaphysics of barbarism.

Palestinians are the simulacrum of the world. The political fate of Palestinians and the moral predicament of our humanity at large are now forever intertwined. The task of recasting the moral and political imaginary of the world from the ruins of Gaza against the dangerous delusion of "Western philosophy" has now just started. In my previous work, I have sought to dismantle the historical roots of the illusion of "the West."[20] We now need to overcome its pernicious phantom of moral and epistemological relevance.

The very moral foundation of Kantian metaphysics is immoral. The philosophical grandfather of Heidegger and Habermas was protesting too much when he wrote that one should act as if one's behavior is a measure of universal behavior. How could racism be considered universal? It is European, not universal. We the people of the world outside Hegelian, Kantian, and, by extension, Western philosophical prose must come to terms with the fact that we are all "inhuman animals," as Israelis call Palestinians and the rest of us who stand by them. And, as such, we have no place, no room, no existential ontology in that philosophical system. We falsely and in astounding ignorance took their universal claims at face value and presumed they were talking about us too. We did not have to wait for Gaza to realize they were not. We need to go back to Kant and the rest of what calls itself "Western philosophy" and recall how Kant spoke of an African in one of his most significant texts, *Observations on the Feeling of the Beautiful and Sublime* (1764):

> Father Labat reports that a Negro carpenter, whom he reproached for haughty treatment towards his wives, answered: "You whites are indeed fools, for first you make great concessions to your wives, and afterward you complain when they drive you mad." And it might be that there were something in this which perhaps deserved to be considered; but in short, this fellow was very black from head to foot, a clear proof that what he said was stupid.[21]

If This Is a Palestinian

> *The boisterous crowds danced and chanted Jewish religious songs outside Damascus Gate as scores of Israeli police stood guard. In several cases, groups chanted slogans such as "Death to Arabs," "Mohammed is Dead" and "May Your Village Burn" as they stared at Palestinian onlookers. Some of the youths wore clothing identifying themselves as members of Lehava—a far-right Jewish supremacist group that opposes assimilation or romantic relationships between Jews and Palestinians.[22]*
>
> PBS News (May 18, 2023)

The facts, histories, and memories of genocide are all around us. Scholars and critical thinkers continue to excavate archives and document genocides around the world. The Jewish Holocaust perpetrated by Nazis must always remain central to our awareness of the darkest chapters in European history, for entirely legitimate reasons. But it was not the only act of genocide in history—it is one among many others equally horrific, equally frightful genocides that Europeans have perpetrated around the world before and after what they did to their own Jewish populations. But why recall? For what purpose?

"As an account of atrocities, therefore," wrote Primo Levi early in his seminal testimonial about the Jewish Holocaust, "this book of mine adds nothing to what is already known to readers throughout the world on the disturbing question of the death camps. It has not been written in order to formulate new accusations; it should be able, rather, to furnish documentation for a quiet study of certain aspects of the human mind."[23] What aspects of the "human mind" might those be exactly? Here is the crux of Levi's point:

> Many people—many nations—can find themselves holding, more or less wittingly, that "every stranger is an enemy." For the most part this conviction lies deep down like some latent infection; it betrays itself only in random, disconnected acts, and does not lie at the base of a system of reason. But when this does come about, when the unspoken dogma becomes the major premise in a syllogism, then, at the end of the chain, there is the Lager. Here is the product of a conception of the world carried rigorously to its logical conclusion; so long as the conception subsists, the conclusion remains to threaten us. The story of the death camps should be understood by everyone as a sinister alarm-signal.

Have we been listening to those alarm-signals? Here is a summary of what Israelis did in Gaza, according to a reasonable and cool-headed official at the UN, Sigrid Kaag, senior humanitarian and reconstruction coordinator for Gaza, some eight months after Israel began its deliberate act of genocide:

> In Gaza . . . over 34,000 people have been killed, and tens of thousands have been injured or maimed. Livelihoods, homes, schools and hospitals have been destroyed.
> The health infrastructure in Gaza has been decimated. The few hospitals still standing struggle to operate due to severe shortages of supplies and frequent power outages. As summer draws near and temperatures rise, communicable diseases threaten to sweep through Gaza.
> Children, who in every crisis suffer the worst and the most, are deprived of nutrition, protection and education, their futures hanging in the balance.
> The scarcity of food and other essential goods has also led to a breakdown in civil order and the gradual unraveling of the social fabric in Gaza. There is no effective law enforcement.[24]

Palestinians are a mostly defenseless people occupied by a massive military might. This is genocide. The world is capable of reading its liberation far beyond the European savageries that, from Hegel and Kant to Levinas and Habermas, their philosophy has sought to sugarcoat and universalize. We have our own signposts to follow and defiant wisdom to share. We have the Palestinian revolutionary Ghassan Kanafani's "Letter from Gaza" (1956), which opens this way:

> Dear Mustafa, I have now received your letter, in which you tell me that you've done everything necessary to enable me to stay with you in Sacramento. I've also received news that I have been accepted in the department of Civil Engineering in the University of California. I must thank you for everything, my friend. But it'll strike you as rather odd when I proclaim this news to you—and make no doubt about it, I feel no hesitation at all, in fact I am pretty well positive that I have never seen things so clearly as I do now. No, my friend, I have changed my mind. I won't follow you to "the land where there is greenery, water and lovely faces" as you wrote. No, I'll stay here, and I won't ever leave.[25]

We are on the cusp of a radically different conception of the world, a conception that has no East or West but opens its protective wings to embrace the entirety of this fragile earth, a conception that reactionary and liberal forces of the status quo seek desperately to demonize, scandalize, and dismiss before it has even dared to reveal itself. The fact that Jews, young and old, are integral to this liberation deeply troubles and upsets the Zionists. We cannot leave any vital voice behind. This is no longer the banality of evil, as Hannah Arendt famously said about Nazism. This is the barefaced vulgarity of evil. We must resist it in moral, imaginative, aesthetic, and epistemic terms. The Palestinian genocide, with Gaza as its epicenter, demands a change in the very foundations of how we see the world from this point onward.

CHAPTER 1

Palestine Is the World; the World Is Palestine

From the River to the Sea, Palestine Will Be Free!
Palestinian solidarity chant

Several chants became proverbial as thousands marched for Palestine around the world. We have heard many shout, "In our thousands, in our millions, we are all Palestinians!" These are noble words, but are they true?[1] Palestinians within Israel have a different experience than Palestinians in Gaza or the West Bank, or the Palestinians in refugee camps in Syria, Lebanon, or Jordan. The fragmentation of the Palestinian national struggle before and after 1948, 1967, the two Intifadas, and now a genocide should be clearly understood before its totality can be grasped, let alone universalized.

The slogan "From the River to the Sea" has a different set of resonances. Zionists use this phrase to mean that they want to conquer the land between the River Jordan to the Mediterranean Sea for themselves, as a military base for an even "Greater Israel," and to exterminate Palestinians in the process. Palestinians, however, use the phrase differently. For Palestinians, the river Jordan to the Mediterranean Sea is their homeland, which they wish to liberate from apartheid and occupation. Critical thinkers, both Palestinian, like the late Edward Said, and Israeli, like Ilan Pappé, have been thinking of a one-state solution that includes both Palestinians and Israelis from the same river to the same sea.[2]

But there is still a different, more potent, more liberating way of reading the slogan. Consider Palestine a river whose struggles against conquest and colonialism for self-determination pour into a sea that is a world with similar if not identical aspirations. This reading of the phrase raises certain questions. Where, in the world, is Palestine? Where might we locate and define Palestine as a floating signifier? We need to ask what is particular and what is universal about Palestine—without disregarding its particularity to a fake universality.

We might place Palestine at the epicenter of our global thinking on "the West versus the Rest." We might see Palestine as the factual and metaphoric simulacrum of the world at large, a world at the mercy of the barbaric logic of "the West" as a talisman of predatory conquest and colonization. Palestine is neither the first nor the last homeland that the West has conquered and abused, but the history of the world has been summarized in Palestine. What Israel is doing in Palestine today is what the world has endured from Western colonialism and imperialism for centuries.

In a review of Timothy Brennan's *Places of Mind: A Life of Edward Said* (2021), Esmat Elhalaby takes serious objection to Said being identified as a "New York intellectual," instead insisting that Said was a global intellectual. Elhalaby points out that "many reviewers of Timothy Brennan's new biography of Said, *Places of Mind*, have taken the opportunity to domesticate the late Palestinian writer. Said is characterized as a representative of precisely those New York intellectuals who regularly derided him. In the *London Review of Books*, Adam Shatz goes to great lengths to argue that Said doesn't "resemble Gramsci or Fanon so much as Susan Sontag."[3] On the contrary, Elhalaby writes, "It was precisely Said's participation in a global political movement—his regular, public refusal to abide by the dictates of the United States' imperial way of life—that drew the ire of so many during his lifetime. Before their recent reinvention, liberal journals such as the *New Republic* and *Dissent* regularly found column inches to attack Said's thought and personage."[4]

So, was Said, in fact, the last Jewish intellectual, as he himself once put it, of the New York vintage, or was he a world intellectual, someone engaged in "a global political movement," as Elhalaby puts it? The fact, of course, is that Said lived much of his prolific life in New York, as a prominent professor at Columbia University. Like millions of other Palestinians, he had found a home outside his homeland, though always slightly out of place, as he describes in his autobiography. "World" is a potent metaphor. "World" is not a place where you arrive after a tiring day at work, hang your hat, sit for dinner with your family, and play a piece of music, as Said did just a few buildings down from where I live. Said was at home nowhere, but his home was in New York, on Columbia's campus. He did belong to that global movement that found itself at home in the world, but he did so from New York. The world, in that metaphoric sense, to which Said belonged, was neither American nor global. It was a Palestinian world—it was *the* Palestinian world.

Palestine as an Epistemological Question

The question of Palestine is first and foremost a political question. A European settler colony that calls itself "Israel" was planted on historic Palestine. It has laid a false claim to it by virtue of *pretending* to privilege one particular Palestinian community, the Jews, casting a universal claim to the entirety of Palestine, which is not entirely Jewish, Islamic, Christian, or any other sectarian denomination. Palestinian Jews have always had and should always have a home in

Palestine. Palestinian Jews are Palestinians—as are Christian and Muslim Palestinians. That simple fact is distorted by Zionists in order to establish the ideological foundations of a settler colony in the entirety of Palestine exclusively for themselves. The idea of a "Jewish state" in Palestine is as much untenable and violent as an "Islamic republic of Palestine," or a "Christian republic of Palestine." But such simple facts are entirely irrelevant to the Zionist project that has taken both Palestinian lands and the Jewish faith hostage to install itself as a European settler colony. During the Suez Canal Crisis of 1956, Israel was put immediately to colonial use by its European founders and benefactors Britain and France to facilitate their invasion of Egypt and oppose the nationalization of the Suez Canal. Zionism was never a project unto itself. It has always been integral to the European, and now American, colonial and imperial projects in the region and beyond. That Jews have been persecuted throughout European history, that Jews need to live in peace anywhere in the world, including Palestine, is entirely irrelevant to the settler-colonial project of European Zionism.[5]

But the political aspect of the Palestinian question should not conceal its other equally important dimensions. Among other things, Palestine also poses a problem for the European and North American modus operandi of knowledge production. Where exactly is the place of Palestine (occupied as it is by a European settler colony) in the leading theoretical and intellectual projects of the European conceptualization of "the World"? Take the idea of "World Literature," for example, or "World Cinema," or "World Music," or "World Religion," or any such project or body of work that begins with the word "World." Do Palestinians, and Palestine as their homeland, have a place in such a world? Are Ghassan Kanafani or Mahmoud Darwish or Fadwa Tuqan, part of World Literature? Liberal professors of comparative literature on North American or European or even Arab campuses might rush to say, "Yes, of course, they are part of world literature."[6] But such a liberal incorporation of Palestinian literature into World Literature, or Palestinian cinema into World Cinema, ipso facto questions the epistemological foregrounding of all those worldly claims. The liberal ecumenicalism of World Literature camouflages that epistemological flaw by way of extending the lifespan of an outdated concept.[7] Palestine problematizes the "World" attached to any moral, political, literary, artistic, or aesthetic claim to universality.

Why is that the case? Again, let us take the example of what is called "World Literature." A leading theorist of World Literature, David Damrosch proposes that "world literature is an elliptical refraction of national literatures."[8] This might be a fine working definition for its immediate and limited purposes on North American university campuses and corresponding undergraduate courses on World Literature. But Persian, Arabic, Hebrew, Sanskrit, or Turkish literatures are not merely "national literatures" awaiting their liberal induction into World Literature. They have a world of their own entirely lost in this imperial assumption of World Literature. Let us therefore set aside the fact that this flawed definition categorically disregards the varied *worlds* in which these "national literatures" already form before they are cannibalized and implicated in this imperial conception of World Literature. What I am interested in is whether Palestinian literature qualifies even as a "national literature" when the very formation of the Palestinian nation has been violently interrupted by the very imperial and colonial projects that initially theorized the idea of World Literature. In much of the presumed dialogue between postcolonial theories and World Literature, the operating words are "post-" and "World." Still under brutal colonial occupation, Palestine is neither "postcolonial" nor of "the World" in which its literature, cultures, cinema, art, music can be located. This epistemic (and political) impossibility of Palestine to be part of "the World" implied in World Literature or World Cinema or World Music does not pose itself as a problem for Palestine, but most certainly does for the worldly claims of those disciplines and regimes of knowledge production that cannot have room for Palestine.

Now consider the peculiarity that "World Literature" does not include Europe or the West. "The West" remains a world of its own. "The West" is the knowing subject of "World Literature." "The World" is the knowable world at the disposal of this European (American) knowing subject. A key issue in the configuration of this idea of "the World" has always been the fact that it bypasses the thorny issue of coloniality. Former colonies in other parts of Asia, Africa, or Latin America might be called "postcolonial" and incorporated into World Literature. But, again, the fact of Palestine raises serious and thorny questions about "the World" that the project of World Literature claims as its domain of theorization. Again, is Palestine part of that world? Do the works of writers like Ghassan Kanafani, Mahmoud Darwish, Emile Habibi, Adania Shibli, and so many others come under the rubric of World Literature, or even "national literature"? If so, in what forms and in what capacities?[9] The abstract debate between World Literature theorists and postcolonial theorists falls flat on its face when we come to Palestinian literature. Palestine is the Achilles' heel of any claim to the "World" in "World Literature"—or any other false universalization that cannot contain Palestine as a bleeding wound of Western colonial projects.

The issue is not just to find problems with the existing paradigms of knowledge production that are by definition Eurocentric and, as such, appear patently flawed when exposed to a healthy dose of criticism. Rather, we need to shift the axis of the world in which we think. The question of Palestine is a political issue with serious epistemological consequences.[10] If we shift the location of such claims to Palestine itself, its historical and phenomenological realities, then we need to start working with such ideas as Nakba/Catastrophe, Intifada/Uprising, Sumud/Resistance. Working through these three specifically Palestinian concepts—Nakba, Intifada, and ultimately Sumud—brings us to current debates on decoloniality, particularly to the leading Latin American theorists of the idea, from Aníbal Quijano (1928–2018) to Walter Mignolo. Palestine here is no longer a passive site of resistance but an active loci of knowledge production and transformative power.[11] Simply saying that Israel is a settler colony is true, but it is not sufficient. We need to place Palestine, not its occupiers, at the epicenter of active transformation of our reading of the world—through such an interface, Palestine and the world become one and the same modus operandi of knowledge production. We must stop thinking of Palestinians as only victims of a brutish colonial project and start thinking of Palestinians as the moral and normative agents of a whole different historiography.

The location of Palestine in the world is synonymous with the location of Palestinians in the world, whether they live in their ancestral homeland inside the Israeli settler colony, or in occupied territories, or in refugee camps, or in Arab capitals, or in any other country around the globe. Perhaps Said's autobiography, *Out of Place* (1999), is a good place to start coming to terms with the amorphous topography of where Palestine is located in the world. Equally crucial is understanding his seminal book, *Orientalism* (1978), as what elsewhere I have called a "renegade text." These are texts that, like their authors, are out of place, texts that are against the epistemologies that occasioned them. The Palestinian cause is, therefore, not just the struggle of one people for their homeland. In that struggle, Palestinians have crafted *a world* of their own, a world we all enter to reimagine the struggles of all ages coming to our contemporary worldliness. In this world, Palestine is one sustained course of reality that refuses to dissolve into the overriding semiosis of the society of spectacles, and consistently generates and sustains its own contrapuntal worldliness. Without Palestine, the project of decoloniality and postcoloniality will always remain an unfinished project. Not European and Eurocentric modernity, as Habermas would surmise, but decolonization as an unfinished project. Palestine, as an epistemological site of anticolonial contestation, is the agent and the occasion of completing that project.[12]

Palestine as a Site of Contestation

Palestine, the ancestral homeland of contemporary Palestinians, is the site of contestation between the European imperial imagination and its colonial consequences that Zionism now exemplifies.[13] The condition of Palestinian coloniality reveals the more global conception of "the West and the Rest," a fiction that needs to metaphorically and physically reassert itself. The shakier its epistemic validity, the more blatant its acts of political violence. Settler colonialism is a condition of impermanence, when everything is in a state of suspension, when things are about to change. This reality blocks any way of coming to terms with a trustworthy conception of a world that dismantles the fiction of "the West and the Rest."

Israel is the latest vindictive brutality of "the West" against "the Rest," genocidally staged in Palestine. Both the occupier and the occupied, the colonizer and the colonized, know and live with the fact that the status quo is untenable. This untenability has lasted for over two centuries in the form of European colonization and decades on the Palestinian premise—but it has never been routinized, accepted, lived with, internalized. As a settler colony, Israel is as unstable as the delusion of "the West." Its European and American enablers must rely on brute military force and vulgar political violence to sustain a fiction of invulnerability. As a façade for the West, Israel must overcompensate violently for what it cannot argue reasonably. What it lacks in logic it seeks to procure through brute violence. It thus self-projects and turns Palestinians and their supporters into insane fanatical terrorists. But Palestinians have no such delusions. Every day they live their Nakba again. Palestine has, therefore, become a perfect metaphor—and this is both its power and its predicament. Palestine has become a repository of all global conditions of anticolonial struggles and the prospects of a decisive decoloniality. Palestine today carries the world historic burden of dismantling in its daily reality the routinized brutality of European coloniality.[14] Nelson Mandela's famous saying "We know too well that our freedom is incomplete without the freedom of the Palestinians," assumes a whole different meaning when we wed the liberation of Palestine to the actively delayed defiance of postcolonial nations to free themselves from domestic tyranny and Western hegemony at one and the same time.[15] This is the umbilical cord linking Palestine to the world.

Palestine, as both a landscape and a metaphor, has become the epicenter of the global struggle against the condition of coloniality, just as Zionism has become the destination of European settler colonialism, and with it the delusional violence of the West. The rise of xenophobic and protofascist politics in Europe and the US all point to a sustained course of coloniality as the modus operandi of imperial knowledge production. Opposing it should never be an equally fictitious myth of "originality." Palestinians are Palestinians not merely by virtue of a counterclaim to the Zionists as to who was there first, Jews or Palestinians. That is a false choice and a rigged game in which both Jews and Palestinians lose. There are Palestinian Jews, and therefore Jewish Palestinians—Jews who have been born and raised in historical Palestine. We must, therefore, consider Palestinians as Palestinians not merely as the native inhabitants of Palestine but equally importantly by virtue of their sustained course of struggle for their homeland and the refusal to be dispossessed and dominated. If there were no such thing as Palestinians in the mind of Israeli warlord Golda Meir, there were Palestinians by virtue of a sustained and principled response to that obscenity. The encounter between the Zionists and the Palestinians is the encounter between the colonizer and the colonized, the settler and the native, "the West" and "the Rest," the occupier and the occupied, the imperial European project to conquer and claim and the anti-imperial Palestinian project to resist conquest and reclaim the land and its living and organic culture. That culture is not merely Palestinian music, or dress, or cuisine, which Zionists are also trying to steal and appropriate. That culture is a culture of resistance, a poem of Mahmoud Darwish, a short story of Ghassan Kanafani, a film by Elia Suleiman, a work of art by Mona Hatoum, a critical essay by Edward Said. Whatever Israelis produce is in the context of European settler colonial conquest, and whatever Palestinians produce points in the opposite direction. Being Palestinian, therefore, is a phenomenological proposition and not a biological or even political speculation.

Everything about Palestine is mythic and allegorical yet all too real. Palestine has become a metaphor in its own terms. Palestine has become the measure of truth, the flag bearer of justice—for the world to bear witness. Heroic sacrifices, visionary resistances, persistent acts of defiance, the refusal to submit to the barefaced armed robbery of their homeland—the enormity of the historic injustice perpetrated against Palestinians has culminated in a struggle and moral victory of mythic proportions. The transmutation of Palestine from fact to a phenomenon is predicated on its worldly disposition as a microcosm of a colonial condition that points far beyond itself. Indigenous people in the US; Inuit, Métis, and First Nations people in Canada; Australian Aboriginal and Torres Strait Islander peoples; Māori people of New Zealand have all been subjugated to the ruling European regimes of conquest and colonization. In Palestine, a pluralistic nation simply refuses to be dominated by the violent European ideology of genocidal Zionism.

Ghassan Kanafani: Palestine as Fact and Phenomenon

How do factual and perhaps even mundane aspects of Palestinian lives become *emblematic* of a possible future? Let's look at the case of a Palestinian revolutionary, his Danish wife and comrade, and an Italian filmmaker. This triangulation embraces *the world* into which the fact and phenomenon of Palestine is placed at the epicenter of our consciousness. This is a case where the microcosm of Palestine becomes allegorical to the macrocosmic frame of all its references. A close examination of this case links the microcosmic and macrocosmic reflections of Palestine and the world onto a semiotic force field, where the ethics, politics, and aesthetics of being (in Palestine) come together. If "Palestine" is not just the liberated name of a homeland, which it is, but also the coded reference to a world that is defined by struggle, then to be a "Palestinian" means something beyond just being born to a Palestinian parent within or outside of Palestine. When a Palestinian icon, his Danish comrade, and her Italian biographer come together, Palestine finds a new global significance, a new worldly disposition.

In the pantheon of Palestinian heroes, Ghassan Kanafani (1936–1972) has a particularly powerful place. His name today personifies Palestine. Kanafani was a leading Palestinian critical thinker, writer, and revolutionary activist. On July 8, 1972, he was assassinated by the Israelis in Beirut, Lebanon. He was survived by his wife Anni Kanafani (née Høver) and their two children. He lived a short life, only thirty-six when he was assassinated, and yet left an indelible mark on the history of the Palestinian struggle.[16] Anni Kanafani was born and raised in Denmark. In 1960, she attended a conference in Yugoslavia where she met a few Palestinian students and was drawn to the Palestinian cause. She subsequently traveled to Lebanon, where she met Ghassan Kanafani and soon their political solidarity blossomed into love and they were married. The Israeli assassination of Kanafani left his young wife widowed with two young children. Anni Kanafani stayed in Beirut. To this day, she continues her work with refugee Palestinian children and runs the Ghassan Kanafani Cultural Foundation. The short but fruitful life of Ghassan and Anni Kanafani together is an iconic emblem where the amorphous topography of Palestine best locates itself. It locates itself in a small gallery at the heart of Mar Elias refugee camp in Beirut, where I met Anni Kanafani for the first time, and where she keeps the memory of her husband and the cause of Palestine alive.

Ordinarily, Anni Kanafani would be a relic of the past, a memory of a leading Palestinian revolutionary. Someone who reminds you of someone else. But in her collaboration with an attentive and competent artist, she becomes something else, she is herself, who she has always been, not a relic but a reality, not a memory but a truth.

9

I met Mario Rizzi for the first time in Liverpool, UK, where we were both attending an art festival. Over the last decade or so, I have studied Rizzi's body of work from various angles, discovering his extraordinary patience, poise, and contemplative camerawork. During one of my visits to Berlin, where Rizzi lives, I brought the significance of Anni Kanafani to his attention.[17] What Rizzi subsequently discovered in her gracious company is the very soul of her lifework, the quintessence of her character. What brings Mario Rizzi,

Anni Kanafani, and Ghassan Kanafani together is not just Palestine as a fact but Palestine as a phenomenon, as a world, enabled and peopled by a nation demanding their pride of place. Palestinians are Muslims, Christians, and Jews, and as such have their own respective holy books. But the sacred certitude of their national liberation movement has crafted a whole different moral universe in which they and their kindred souls dwell. The indwelling of people as different as a Danish woman, an Italian filmmaker, and a Palestinian iconic hero is precisely where Palestine has a place in the world yet to be fathomed in Eurocentric World Literature or World Cinema.

Mario Rizzi's films in general are studies in border crossing. In such crosscurrents of history, geography, and cultures, Rizzi always sees hidden and untold stories. He sees and hears those stories otherwise unseen and unheard by others. He has an urge, like a dreamer, to show and tell those stories. In *The Little Lantern* (2019), Rizzi goes to the heart of a tumultuous national consciousness to tell a story everyone knows but no one has yet told in its hidden truths. Anni Kanafani's story was so obvious, so evident, that it was hiding in plain sight. In her presence, *being Palestinian* becomes a transnational phenomenon precisely by the storytelling sensibilities that an Italian filmmaker and a Danish surrogate for the truth of the Palestinian cause bring together. Palestine is blessed with countless gifted filmmakers—from Ibrahim Hassan Sirhan (1915–1987) to Michel Khleifi to Mai Masri to Elia Suleiman—telling their own stories from a variety of angles. That is the gift of Palestinian cinema for the world at large. What Mario Rizzi and Anni Kanafani bring to Ghassan Kanafani's story is the reciprocal gift of the world back to Palestine—where Palestine finds its worldly place and where the world opens a space for Palestine.

The Fertile Memory of Palestine

Mario Rizzi's take on Ghassan and Anni Kanafani does not happen in a vacuum. In a masterpiece of Palestinian cinema, Michel Khleifi's *Fertile Memory* (1980), we encounter the parallel lives of two Palestinian women, Farah Hatoum, a widow in her fifties, and Sahar Khalifeh, a young writer and teacher in the Israeli-occupied West Bank, where the anodyne realities of their daily lives become the substance of truths otherwise hidden under the bombastic slogans of one sort or another. In *Women Without Men* (2009), a novella by Shahrnush Parsipur that was subsequently turned into a movie by Shirin Neshat, we encounter the lives of four women living in Tehran in 1953, as the CIA coup to topple Mohammad Mosadegh is under way. In such landmark works of art, the camera begins to look at history from its invisibilized perspectives. Mario Rizzi's *The Little Lantern* has such a revelatory angle to its quiet preoccupations.

The visual memory of the Palestinian predicament as both fact and phenomenon resonates with the world in which it unfolds, the world it helps locate on the map. The artwork thus becomes the microcosm of the world that embraces and informs it—and there and then calls it "Palestine," not by virtue of a mere geographical history but by virtue of an emotive universe otherwise hidden to the naked eye.

Palestinian stories are hard to tell for the simple fact that Palestinian lives overwhelm any mimetic method to represent them.[18] *The Little Lantern* is a Palestinian story, told by an Italian artist about a Danish woman who has devoted her life to the cause and then the memory of her husband. How does one tell such a story? The camera must first learn humility, then master the art of chasing after fragmented truths in the winding alleys of Palestinian refugee camps in Beirut. How does Mario Rizzi tell his story? There are four components to Rizzi's *Little Lantern*—woven together with precision and elegance: the first is the preparation for a play that a group of children are about to perform, the second is the play itself, the third is the labyrinth of Palestinian refugee camps where this play (and Rizzi's film) is taking place, and the fourth is, of course, the story Anni Kanafani tells us about her life and dedication to Palestinian children in the camps. There, in a nutshell, is the world Palestine creates and in which Palestine is located, not just a dot on any map, but the emotive universe into which the material world dissolves.

The first two elements and the second two components in Rizzi's film come together and dissolve into each other smoothly—but each half could be a film of its own. Both parts are connected with Rizzi's signature grace. What holds the two films together are the narrow and winding streets and alleys of the Palestinian refugee camps, where the architectonics of a terrorizing injustice has given itself a monumental edifice to mark and to remember itself. I have walked those winding alleys of Sabra and Shatila and other Palestinian refugee camps with friends and comrades, from Lebanon to Syria. Pay close attention to Rizzi's camerawork through these streets and alleys. These shots will hold you and the film together. Rizzi shows us that to be a witness to the Palestinian truth is at once liberating and absolving, and in that liberation and absolution dwells the microcosm of the Palestinian world, without which no other world can become worldly.

What is the play the children in Maro Rizzi's film are enacting? Ghassan Kanafani's "Al-Qandil al-Saghir / The Little Lantern" was written for and dedicated to his niece Lamis, for her eighth birthday.[19] When Kanafani died in that car bomb, the explosion claimed the life of his beloved niece Lamis as well. The play is the story of a king who, upon his death, leaves his throne to his daughter, telling her she will become a queen when she brings the sun to their castle. The little princess climbs mountains and sets a lucrative prize for whoever brings her the sun. An old man walks into the castle with a lantern but he is turned away. The old man sends a message to the princess: "How could you house the sun in your castle when you don't have room for a small lantern?" The princess learns the wisdom of those words and orders the walls of the castle to be brought down. All people are invited into her castle. Everyone brings a little lantern, at which moment she realizes her father's wish, not the sun in the sky but small lanterns that come together to shine like a sun. She was the queen of the people. From the mind of Ghassan Kanafani, to the noble dedication of Anni Kanafani, to the camerawork of Mario Rizzi, those little lanterns have become emblematic of the world that Palestine as a fact and Palestine as a cause has created and sustained.

There are some significant changes that Mario Rizzi has introduced to Ghassan Kanafani's story when he stages it in his film. In Kanafani's book, it is an old man who walks into the castle with a lantern, but in Rizzi's play it is a woman, who in turn, on behalf of the people, crowns the queen. All the children in Rizzi's play are actual students in Anni Kanafani's kindergarten or the graduates of the kindergarten in Burj el-Barajneh Camp. They are the fourth generation of refugees who were forced to leave Palestine in 1948. Since 1974, more than ten thousand children have graduated from Ghassan Kanafani Cultural Foundation kindergartens. What we watch in the movie is an *assemblage* of a living memory of Nakba woven into the very fabric of the world Palestine has occasioned and occupied across cultural boundaries and colonial borders. The issue of Palestine as an epistemological proposition is not resolved by the "generosity" of the liberal imaginations of those who theorize on World Literature or World Cinema in the US or Europe. It is resolved here—right at the heart of a Palestinian refugee camp where the widow of Kanafani expands his aesthetics of resistance.

That minor variation between the text and the paratext, however, is not the only difference we notice between Ghassan Kanafani's story and Mario Rizzi's film. Kanafani was a socialist revolutionary. The significance of his story is both sweet and simple. But how are we to read it in conjunction with the story that Anni Kanafani is telling us, and then with the story that Rizzi is telling us? The ultimate interlocutor of all these stories is Lamis. That murdered Palestinian child for whom "The Little Lantern" was originally written can no longer read, listen, or watch—and yet she is the ultimate interlocutor of Anni Kanafani's love story and Mario Rizzi's filmic homage. Rizzi too dedicates his film to Lamis. Anni Kanafani now speaks with the voice of a murdered eight-year-old Palestinian child, having devoted all her life to thousands of other little Lamises in Palestinian refugee camps. We have by now exited the material world of a settler colony imposing its military rule over a defiant nation. We are, by now, in the open border world that Lamis's memory has occasioned and sustained.

With so many murdered Lamises as observant, but silent, interlocutors, Rizzi is sharing with us the dilemma of how to tell the story of the widow of a monumental, larger-than-life hero of the Palestinian cause. In two ways, Anni Kanafani is an outsider insider. She is a white Danish woman, Anni Høver, married to a mythic Palestinian martyr. Where is she, where would she be located—in what world, what habitat? She, of course, proudly carries the last name of her husband, Kanafani. But under the guise of that iconic name, where does Anni Kanafani end and Anni Høver begin? Are these two different people? Does our calling her by her maiden name resolve the issue? She has lived a long, rich, fulfilling, and honorable life as Anni Kanafani. Calling her Anni Høver erases that history. The task Rizzi faced was to tell the story of Anni Kanafani as who and what and why she is, without reducing her back to who she was before she married Ghassan Kanafani or simply as his widow. What sustains the fact and the phenomenon of Anni Kanafani as a Palestinian icon is precisely the world she inhabits and the memories she personifies.

In telling us her story with Ghassan Kanafani, while an iconic story of Ghassan Kanafani is being staged by her schoolchildren, Anni Kanafani becomes the storyteller where and when her husband has become silenced. In her gracefully aging countenance, we can see the eight-year-old Lamis listening and watching. Ghassan Kanafani has become silenced, yet his little allegory has now found a different storyteller—Anni Kanafani, as shown by Mario Rizzi. This is where Rizzi excels, and this is where a "wife" finds her own voice as a woman, a person, with autonomy to tell us her story—giving a new meaning to the "Kanafani" in her name. The relationship between Ghassan Kanafani's story and Anni Kanafani's story becomes emblematic of the relationship between Ghassan Kanafani and Anni Kanafani—doubling and splitting what it means to be a "Kanafani." The interface does not efface the marital relationship but transcends it. Everyone knows Ghassan Kanafani, and everyone knows Anni Kanafani as his wife. But how does, and how can, Anni Kanafani begin to talk in a manner that is her own voice, the totality of her voice, as a Danish woman, as a student activist, as a person committed to justice and the Palestinian cause, as a lover, then a wife, then a mother, then a bereaved widow, and then as a selfless educator committed to the education of Palestinian and other refugee children. In and around the Kanafanis, when the husband and wife mirror each other in Rizzi's camera and become one, Palestine opens up a new radically defiant conception of the world they inhabit. Any and all ideas of the world—literature, cinema, philosophy, and so forth—must begin with this specific site and build itself up around the world.

The Idea of a Palestinian

Who is a Palestinian? Where is a Palestinian? Where in the world is Palestine? What in the world might we mean when we say, "We are all Palestinians?" A Palestinian is a person born in Palestine, or to Palestinian parents inside or outside of Palestine. But generations of anticolonial struggles have also made Palestine a moral imperative. You might say Anni Kanafani has become an honorary Palestinian, at home now among homeless people, herself a refugee transplanted by her consciousness in their midst, in the heart of a refugee camp, or more accurately, a constellation of refugee camps. The fusion of fact and fiction in Mario Rizzi's film is where Palestine finds its enduring universe. Edward Said belonged to this universe. Like countless other Palestinians, Edward Said was and remains neither a New York intellectual, nor a world intellectual. He was and he remains a Palestinian intellectual. He was part of a struggle that made Palestine worldly by universalizing its particulars. He lived in New York and he was celebrated around the world as what and who he always was: a Palestinian.

Examples such as Anni Kanafani or Mario Rizzi are not a simple case of "solidarity" with the Palestinian cause, which might be here today and gone tomorrow. Their story is the story of how Palestinians become metaphoric at the very moment of storytelling. Mario Rizzi is an Italian artist who lives in Germany and is drawn to the lives and circumstances of refugees, outcasts, pariahs, the subaltern anywhere in the world. To tell the story of a Danish woman in Palestinian refugee camps, he has employed the best of his artistic capacities and the result has brought him home to other iconic moments in Palestinian history. There is a poem by the Palestinian national poet Mahmoud Darwish (1941–2008) that, after watching Rizzi's film about Anni Kanafani, assumes a whole different meaning. It does not matter if Darwish composed this poem for any particular woman, or for women in general, or for no woman at all. What matters is how the fusion of Rizzi's film about Anni Kanafani and Darwish's poem generate a tertiary space where both the film and the poem come together to take us somewhere else.

> I am a woman. No more and no less
> I live my life as it is
> thread by thread
> and I spin my wool to wear, not
> to complete Homer's story, or his sun.
> And I see what I see
> as it is, in its shape,
> though I stare every once
> in a while in its shade
> to sense the pulse of defeat,
> and I write tomorrow

on yesterday's sheets: there's no sound
other than echo.
I love the necessary vagueness in
what a night traveler says to the absence
of birds over the slopes of speech
and above the roofs of villages
I am a woman, no more and no less

The almond blossom sends me flying
in March, from my balcony,
in longing for what the faraway says:
"Touch me and I'll bring my horses to the water springs."
I cry for no clear reason, and I love you
as you are, not as a strut
nor in vain
and from my shoulders a morning rises onto you
and falls into you, when I embrace you, a night.
But I am neither one nor the other
no, I am not a sun or a moon
I am a woman, no more and no less

So be the Qyss of longing,
if you wish. As for me
I like to be loved as I am
not as a color photo
in the paper, or as an idea

composed in a poem amid the stags . . .
I hear Laila's faraway scream
from the bedroom: Do not leave me
a prisoner of rhyme in the tribal nights
do not leave me to them as news . . .
I am a woman, no more and no less

I am who I am, as
you are who you are: you live in me
and I live in you, to and for you
I love the necessary clarity of our mutual puzzle
I am yours when I overflow the night
but I am not a land
or a journey
I am a woman, no more and no less

And I tire
from the moon's feminine cycle
and my guitar falls ill
string
by string
I am a woman,
no more
and no less![20]

Consider how Darwish's poem might be read in anticipation of Anni Kanafani. Anni Kanafani too is a woman, "no more and no less," who lives her life as it is, "thread by thread," and through Mario Rizzi's film we see how she lives that life "not to complete" Ghassan Kanafani's story but to unfold it metamorphically as her own. Anni Kanafani too has been writing the "tomorrow on yesterday's sheets," but her own sound is not just an echo. Could Ghassan Kanafani have become Ghassan Kanafani without the love and devotion of Anni Kanafani, knowing full well in the mirror of her mind, her heart, and her soul he will continue to live to wage truth to power? There, upon that certainty, Mario Rizzi has enabled Anni Kanafani to declare: "I am a woman, no more and no less." That womanhood, personhood, humanity is enabled and empowered on the site of Palestinian worldliness.

In his film about Anni Kanafani, Mario Rizzi has used the story of one Palestinian hero we know to tell the story of another Danish hero we may not have known. The history of European colonialism has culminated in the project of Zionism to write the Palestinian fact out of history. The singular place of Palestine in the world (before and after Zionism) is to recast the world as epistemically unknowable until and unless Palestinians too have a place in the world. I have opted for a detailed reading of a documentary by an Italian filmmaker about a Danish educator who has graced and been graced by the literary and revolutionary legacy of a martyred, mythic, Palestinian hero. The event and the occasion form the microcosm of how Palestine *is* the world it enables and the world *is* the Palestine it embraces.

CHAPTER 2

Israel Is "the West"; "the West" Is Israel

We declare that Israel's intentional and targeted starvation campaign against the Palestinian people is a form of genocidal violence and has resulted in famine across all of Gaza.[1]
　　UN Special Committee on Israeli Practices
　　in the Occupied Territories (July 9, 2024)

As a settler colony, Israel is a symptom of a moral malady, not the moral malady itself. The Israeli savagery staged during the most recent war on Gaza, but always evident ever since its colonial invention, is not the cause but the symptom of the delusional malaise called "the West." Colonial savagery, rooted in the historical pedigree of the term "the West," defines the contours of the carnage unfolding in Palestine. A settler-colonial project invented by the West as a garrison state is in place to protect its global interests against the encroaching posturing of Russia and China. But such geostrategic readings of the event fail to grasp its momentous barbarism.

The history of Zionist colonization and dispossession is not done yet and still progresses apace. The eminent Israeli historian Ilan Pappé, one of the sharpest and most precise chronicler of the Palestinian predicament, provides a glimpse of the measure of colonization in Palestine. "When the sixth day of the June 1967 war came to an end," he writes, "the State of Israel extended over an area three times larger than its original size and added one million Palestinians to the 300,000 already resident in the state since 1948."[2] Pappé further explains that this "figure was more or less the same number of Palestinians expelled by Israel in 1948. The million doubled, tripled, and continued to grow as the years passed, and reached, together with the Palestinians in Israel, almost five million by the beginning of the twenty-first century."[3] That, is five million Palestinians made into colonial subjects in their own homeland.

"Along with them," Pappé continues, "in more than fifty years of colonization, half a million Jewish settlers have also inhabited vast areas within the Occupied Territories, and as I write [in 2017] they continue to flow in and encroach upon the limited space allotted to the Palestinians." Extracting the most recent genocide in Gaza from this history renders it meaningless. The Palestinian genocide, just like the Jewish Holocaust, will have to be consistently historicized, narrated, chronicled, witnessed, and remembered. The admirable and absolutely necessary recollection of the Jewish Holocaust and, indeed, the very institutions of Yad Vashem must be followed closely in witnessing and commemorating the Palestinian genocide. The two atrocities are interrelated as the two sides of the same coin of European genocidal practices.

In his seminal study, *The Ethnic Cleansing of Palestine* (2006), Pappé set the historical context of this colonization, linking it to the history of European antisemitism and prolonged persecution of the Jewish people:

> Zionism emerged in the late 1880s in central and eastern Europe as a national revival movement, prompted by the growing pressure on Jews in those regions either to assimilate totally or risk continuing persecution (though, as we know, even complete assimilation was no safeguard against annihilation in the case of Nazi Germany). By the beginning of the twentieth century, most of the leaders of the Zionist movement associated this national revival with the colonization of Palestine. Others, especially the founder of the movement, Theodor Herzl, were more ambivalent, but after his death, in 1904, the orientation towards Palestine was fixed and consensual.[4]

In the context of the European hatred of Jews and European colonialism in the world at large, Zionism became the mobilizing ideology of conquest and colonization that brought European colonialism and antisemitism together. What we are witnessing in Palestine is a logical and rhetorical extension of the Jewish Holocaust in Europe, which itself emulated German genocidal practices in Africa—the Herero and Nama genocide of 1904 in what is today the country of Namibia.

A Review of Settler Colonialism

South Africa, mindful of the jus cogens character of the prohibition of genocide and the erga omnes and erga omnes partes character of the obligations owed by States under the Genocide Convention, is making the present application to establish Israel's responsibility for violations of the Genocide Convention; to hold it fully accountable under international law for those violations; and—most immediately—to have recourse to this Court to ensure the urgent and fullest possible protection for Palestinians in Gaza who remain at grave and immediate risk of continuing and further acts of genocide.[5]
Application of the Convention on the Prevention and Punishment of the Crime of Genocide in the Gaza Strip (*South Africa v. Israel*, December 29, 2023)

The phenomenon that connects Israel to the West is settler colonialism. Over the last few decades, there has been a significant rise in critical studies of Israel as a potent example of European settler colonialism. In a pioneering, book-length essay originally written in 1966 and published during the 1967 Arab-Israeli war in Jean-Paul Sartre's signature journal *Les Temps Modernes*, the eminent French scholar Maxime Rodinson (1915–2004) clearly identified Israel as a settler-colonial state. The essay subsequently appeared in English in 1973 and established a solid scholarly basis for seeing Israel for what it is.[6] "I believe," Rodinson concluded in clear, concise, and indisputable prose, "the creation of the State of Israel on Palestinian soil is the culmination of a process that fits perfectly into the great European-American movement of expansion in the nineteenth and twentieth centuries whose aim was to settle new inhabitants among other people or to dominate them economically and politically. This is, moreover, an obvious diagnosis, and if I have taken so many words to state it, it is only because of the separate efforts that have been made to conceal it."[7] Another landmark essay from the same period was penned by the prominent economist Arghiri Emmanuel (1911–2001). Titled "White-Settler Colonialism and the Myth of Investment Imperialism" (1972), this essay further theorized the idea beyond the case of Israel.[8] The point of both these major works was to define settler colonialism as the systematic elimination of local inhabitants and their replacement with a new population.

Scholarship on Israel as a settler colony continues to grow. In a more recent study, "The Other Shift: Settler Colonialism, Israel, and the Occupation" (2013), historian Lorenzo Veracini argues that we have seen a shift "from a border to an ethnic conflict," which amounts to a transition from a system of relationships that can be understood as settler colonial to a relational system crucially characterized by colonial forms.[9] Veracini clarifies the distinction between colonial and settler-colonial formations, arguing that the incompleteness of Israel's settler-colonial project has led to its occupation of Palestine taking on a more classically colonial form. In another major study, "A Century of Settler Colonialism in Palestine: Zionism's Entangled Project," Tariq Dana and Ali Jarbawi identify Israel as "the most sophisticated settler-colonial project of our age."[10] They stipulate that "while this settler-colonial project continues unabated, it is an entangled one, unable to reach the ultimate point of Jewish exclusivity in the land."[11] They too identify the operative logic of settler colonialism as "eliminating the native." At the same time, they rightly identify "the vibrant Palestinian presence in the land, the everyday resistance to the colonial order, and the robust Palestinian adherence to their rights . . . as structural obstacles to the ultimate realization of the 'Zionist dream.'"[12] Zionist settler colonialism is and shall always remain incomplete, as fifteen million Palestinians inside and outside their homeland simply refuse to let go of Palestine.

Central to the project of settler colonialism is, of course, the erasure of the natives. In a widely influential essay, "Settler Colonialism and the Elimination of the Native" (2006), Australian historian Patrick Wolfe (1949–2016) maps out a complete panorama of what happens in the process of active, violent, and racist dispossession of the natives—a map we have seen unfold in Palestine to this day:

> Settler colonialism destroys to replace. As Theodor Herzl, founding father of Zionism, observed in his allegorical manifesto/novel, "If I wish to substitute a new building for an old one, I must demolish before I construct." In a kind of realization that took place half a century later, one-time deputy-mayor of West Jerusalem Meron Benvenisti recalled, "As a member of a pioneering youth movement, I myself 'made the desert bloom' by uprooting the ancient olive trees of al-Bassa to clear the ground for a banana grove, as required by the 'planned farming' principles of my kibbutz, Rosh Haniqra." Renaming is central to the cadastral effacement/replacement of the Palestinian Arab presence that Benvenisti poignantly recounts. . . . The ideological justification for the dispossession of Aborigines was that "we" could use the land better than they

could, not that we had been on the land primordially and were merely returning home.[13]

In another study, equally crucial, "Settler Colonial Logics and the Neoliberal Regime" (2016), David Lloyd and Patrick Wolfe locate settler colonialism in the larger context of globalized capitalism: "In particular, settler colonialism and primitive accumulation have been understood to belong to early stages of capital expansion and accordingly to be formations lodged in the past."[14] But they argue that "the ongoing history of settler colonialism forms a crucial terrain through which to understand military occupation and the formations and practices of the neoliberal state that has emerged to regulate and promote a new regime of accumulation."[15]

The significance of this body of extraordinary scholarship is its comparative dimension, that it does not single out Israel, geographically or historically. In "Zionism as Colonialism: A Comparative View of Diluted Colonialism in Asia and Africa" (2008), a decidedly comparative study, Ilan Pappé argues: "Zionist settlers . . . were motivated by a national impulse but acted as pure colonialists."[16] To make the point more theoretical and compelling, Pappé rightly places Zionism in the context of European global colonialism

> Zionism was not, after all, the only case in history in which a colonialist project was pursued in the

name of national or otherwise noncolonialist ideals. Zionists relocated to Palestine at the end of a century in which Europeans controlled much of Africa, the Caribbean, and other places in the name of "progress" or idealism not unfamiliar to the Zionist movement.[17]

The language of that idealism has been consistent throughout European colonial conquests of the world and is most patently evident in Palestine ever since the Zionist project commenced. Zionism "happened in a century when French settlers colonized Algeria, claiming an atavist and emotional link to the Algerian soil no less profound than the one professed by the early Zionists with regard to Eretz Yisrael."[18] Zionists also fully partook in the "white man burden of civilizing the natives": "Like the Zionists, the colonies built by Europeans in these continents were allegedly for the benefit of the local people. As it turned out, the colonies became imperialist communities serving only the strategic interests of European powers and the settlers themselves. In the period of the white man's penetration into Africa and Asia, the Jews "returned" to their 'homeland.'"[19]

The invention of Israel mimics the invention of the West as the totemic mascot of a globalized capitalism, with its brutish colonial edge. Israel is the microcosm of the West—doing in Palestine what the West has done to the world. Israelis have massacred generations of Palestinians on the blueprint of European colonialists ravaging the earth. To do so with complete impunity, they had to turn Palestinians into knowable objects, into beasts, held inside a zoo, or as mummified inanimate items in a natural history museum.

When citing Kurtz at the end of *Heart of Darkness*, Sven Lindqvist dwells for a moment on the word "exterminate." He writes: "Africans have been called beasts ever since the very first contacts, when Europeans described them as 'rude and beastlie,' 'like to brute beasts,' and 'more brutish than the beasts they hunt.'"[20] Now, read this short paragraph from the Commission of Inquiry on the Occupied Palestinian Territory, dated June 19, 2024:

> In relation to Israel's military operations and attacks in Gaza from 7 October, the Commission concluded that Israeli authorities were responsible for war crimes, crimes against humanity, and violations of international humanitarian and human rights law, including extermination, intentionally directing attacks against civilians, murder or willful killing, using starvation as a method of war, forcible transfer, gender persecution, sexual and gender-based violence amounting to torture, and cruel or inhuman treatment.[21]

Uncritical Theory

After five months of military operations, Israel has destroyed Gaza. Over 30,000 Palestinians have been killed, including more than 13,000 children. Over 12,000 are presumed dead and 71,000 injured, many with life-changing mutilations. Seventy percent of residential areas have been destroyed. Eighty percent of the whole population has been forcibly displaced. Thousands of families have lost loved ones or have been wiped out. Many could not bury and mourn their relatives, forced instead to leave their bodies decomposing in homes, in the street or under the rubble. Thousands have been detained and systematically subjected to inhuman and degrading treatment. The incalculable collective trauma will be experienced for generations to come.[22]

Francesca Albanese, *Anatomy of a Genocide*, Report of the Special Rapporteur on the Situation of Human Rights in the Palestinian Territory Occupied since 1967, UN (March 24, 2024)

Are we morally, theoretically, imaginatively ready to reckon with the Palestinian genocide and to connect it thematically to the Jewish Holocaust? How can we create the critical apparatus we need? We are at a moment of radical epistemic shifts. The tradition of the irredeemably Eurocentric "Critical Theory" deeply disappoints us. Gaza has become a defining trauma of the rest of our humanity. Gaza spells an epistemic shift in our unfolding future.

"Adorno often indulged in the petty-bourgeois politics of complicit passivity," writes Gabriel Rockhill in a critical assessment of Theodor Adorno and Max Horkheimer's ignorance or indifference to the consequences of European colonialism, "avoiding public pronouncements on major political events, the few statements he did make were strikingly reactionary." We need more specific evidence: "For instance, in 1956, he co-authored an article with Horkheimer in defense of the imperialist invasion of Egypt by Israel, Britain and France, which aimed at seizing the Suez Canal and overthrowing Nasser (an action condemned by the United Nations). Referring to Nasser, one of the prominent anti-colonial leaders of the non-aligned movement, as 'a fascist chieftain [...] who conspires with Moscow.'"[23] Here, chapter and verse, we have a record of Adorno and Horkheimer, members of the Frankfurt School and leading philosophers of Critical Theory, aligning with Israel and its Western partners in invading Egypt to retain control of a major strategic passageway. The key word of contempt that Adorno and Horkheimer use here is, of course, "chieftain." The two distinguished German philosophers were writing these words in 1956, after leaving Hitler's Germany, Mussolini's Italy, and

ISRAEL IS "THE WEST"; "THE WEST" IS ISRAEL 43

Franco's Spain to Eisenhower's US. Were any of these Europeans also characterized as a "chieftain"? Why reserve this contemptible word only for an Arab, an African, and a Muslim leader? This damning documentation of Adorno and Horkheimer's support for colonialism is based on the major work of Stuart Jeffries, who had already reported:

> Adorno and his co-director Horkheimer weren't devoid of political commitment when they felt like it. In 1956, for instance, they wrote to the German news magazine *Der Spiegel* to defend France and Britain's military assault on Egypt which had been condemned by the United Nations. "No one even ventures to point out that these Arab robber states have been on the lookout for years for an opportunity to fall upon Israel and to slaughter the Jews who have found refuge there."[24]

The preeminent critical philosophers of the Frankfurt School could not even utter the word "Palestine." It is simply "there." And what exactly was Egypt robbing? Their own territorial sovereignty? As Rockhill puts it: "According to this pseudo-dialectical inversion, it is the Arab states that are 'robbers,' not the settler colony working with core imperialist countries to infringe upon the self-determination of Arabs."[25] Rockhill further adds:

Rather than supporting the global movement for anticolonial liberation and the building of a socialist world, they celebrate—with only a few minor exceptions—the superiority of the West, while repeatedly disparaging the Soviet Union and China. Invoking stock racist descriptions [they describe] the "barbarians" in the East... using the overtly sub-humanizing vocabulary of "beasts" and "hordes."[26]

What to do with Adorno and Horkheimer when caught with their hands in the colonial cookie jar? Critical stances vis-à-vis the Soviet Union and China can be perfectly fine, but not to the pathological degree of aligning with France, the UK, and Israel against a sovereign African nation, Egypt, defending its territorial integrity. Should we, after reading this truly banal position, throw the baby of Critical Theory out with the nauseating racist bathwater? The issue is not limited to historical ignorance of varied degrees but degenerates into vast civilizational proportions. The following exchange between Adorno and Horkheimer in the course of drafting what they call the "New Manifesto" is quite revealing:

Horkheimer: The Western world.

Adorno: We know nothing of Asia.

ISRAEL IS "THE WEST"; "THE WEST" IS ISRAEL   45

Horkheimer: What are we to say to the Western world? You must deliver food to the East?

Adorno: The introduction of fully fledged socialism, Third Phase in the various countries. Everything hinges on that. What about the *Communist Manifesto* as a theme for variations?

Horkheimer: The world situation is that everything seems to be improving, but the world's liberators all look like Cesare Borgia.

Adorno: I have the feeling that, under the banner of Marxism, the East might overtake Western civilization. This would mean a shift in the entire dynamics of history. Marxism is being adopted in Asia in much the same way as Christianity was taken up in Mexico at one time. Europe too will probably be swallowed up at some point in the future.

Horkheimer: I believe that Europe and America are probably the best civilizations that history has produced up to now as far as prosperity and justice are concerned. The key point now is to ensure the preservation of these gains. That can be achieved only if we remain ruthlessly critical of this civilization.

Adorno: We cannot call for the defense of the Western world.

Horkheimer: We cannot do so because that would destroy it.[27]

What is left to be said about Adorno and Horkheimer after this exchange, of their Marxism, post-Marxism, Frankfurt School, or (if you pardon the expression) "Critical Theory"? It is not just that they are racially biased against the world outside their "West." Rather, they do not even see the parts of the world that is outside their claustrophobic circles. As Rockhill notes about the exchange between Horkheimer and Adorno included above:

> This was in 1956, when the U.S. was still largely racially segregated, was involved in anti-communist witch hunts and destabilization campaigns around the world, and had recently extended its imperial reach by overthrowing democratically elected governments in Iran (1953) and Guatemala (1954), while the European powers were waging violent struggles to hold onto their colonies or convert them into neo-colonies.[28]

We therefore need to engage with far more potent critical thinkers. In my work, I have often engaged with, for example, the Argentine philosopher Enrique Dussel. "Central to Dussel's criticism of the Frankfurt School," as Antonio Y. Vázquez-Arroyo puts it, "is its failure to explicitly thematize, let alone conceptualize, colonialism, which he traces to a Eurocentric outlook that consists in never thinking beyond the North Atlantic fold."[29] With thinkers like Dussel and Vázquez-Arroyo, we have surpassed the "Critical Theory" that a provincial generation of European philosophers left behind. Here is Vázquez-Arroyo's concise summation of the significance of Dussel in overcoming the phantom of Eurocentric Critical Theory:

> Enrique Dussel has formulated the most significant engagement with Critical Theory from the perspective of his decolonial philosophy of liberation. . . . Roughly speaking, Dussel's version of epistemological decolonization consists of four core tenets: first, to take critical notice, from the perspective of the postcolonial world, not just of Eurocentrism as a locus of enunciation but also as a habitus that deeply penetrates both the subjectivity of thinkers and the objectivity of the theories these formulate. Second, to call into question the universal claims of European thought and, similarly, the imitation of these thought forms. Third, to debunk "developmental fallacies" inscribed in European thought that at once misrecognize and universalize European paths

of development; and fourth, to formulate knowledge from the peripheries, not the metropolitan centers (like most decolonial thinkers, he takes for granted Immanuel Wallerstein's world systems theory), and thus invert the terms of capitalist modernity.[30]

The most significant recent intervention in this regard is Amy Allen's *The End of Progress: Decolonizing the Normative Foundations of Critical Theory* (2016). Here is how she puts it:

> I believe that there is a reason for the Frankfurt School's failure to respond adequately to the predicaments of our post- and neocolonial world and that this reason is connected to philosophical commitments that run deep in the work of its contemporary practitioners. The problem, as I see it, arises from the particular role that ideas of historical progress, development, social evolution, and sociocultural learning play in justifying and grounding the normative perspective of critical theorists such as Habermas and Honneth.[31]

It is, therefore, impossible today to read Adorno and his generation of Europeanists without seeing them as the rightful descendants of the racist philosophies of Hegel and Kant. Their works have never been sufficient for our critical understanding of the global context. Their blinding Eurocentrism, their unfailing racist preoccupation with "Western Civilization," their numbing indifference to the world at large, and their astonishing ignorance of non-European critical cultures makes them not entirely useless but, in fact, useful as symptoms of the disease they think they want to cure but instead exacerbate. When these "critical thinkers" believed the superiority of the West could be secured and achieved only if they remained "ruthlessly critical" of other civilizations, they, in fact, go even beyond the most reactionary thinkers integral to the racism of "Western philosophy."

When the courageous UN rapporteur Francesca Albanese underlines the fact that in Gaza "the incalculable collective trauma will be experienced for generations to come," we need a far deeper historical and philosophical understanding of where that ideology that calls itself "the West" originates: not in the most reactionary but, rather, in the most critical thinkers of its philosophical tradition.

A Syncretic Palestinian Liberation Theology

The South African Church taught us the concept of the "state theology," defined as "the theological justification of the status quo with its racism, capitalism and totalitarianism." It does so by misusing theological concepts and

> *biblical texts for its own political purposes. Here in Palestine, the Bible is weaponized against us. Our very own sacred text. In our terminology in Palestine, we speak of the Empire. Here we confront the theology of the Empire.*[32]
>
> **Reverend Munther Isaac**, Evangelical Lutheran Christmas Church Bethlehem (Saturday, December 23, 2023)

If Critical Theory has failed to resemble anything like a liberating force, Palestinian and Jewish liberation theologies are in much more poised positions. Critical Theory is today receiving a much-needed corrective push through a liberation philosophy of the sort that Enrique Dussel articulated decades ago.[33] But what about liberation theology?

"We are angry. We are broken. This should have been a time of joy; instead, we are mourning. We are fearful."[34] With these words, Reverend Munther Isaac began his sermon the day before Christmas Eve in 2023 as Israeli forces continued to bomb Gaza. Among the tens of thousands of Palestinians killed were Christians, Muslims, men, women, and children. We scarcely knew their full names let alone their religious denominations.

It is impossible to distinguish between a Muslim and a Christian Palestinian when it comes to their struggles and sacrifices for the liberation of their homeland. When Palestinian journalist Shireen Abu Akleh (1971–2022) was murdered point-blank by the US- and EU-backed occupying forces in

Palestine, the moving iconography of her martyrdom marked her as a Palestinian.[35] The term "Palestinian" itself has by now assumed its own metaphysical power, a civil theological potency, irreducible to Christian or Islamic denominators. Reverend Isaac's sermon is a key passage in what we might consider a "Palestinian liberation theology," which stands in stark contrast to the Evangelical Zionism that has laid a settler-colonial claim on Christianity as it aids and abets the conquest of Palestine. While this Palestinian liberation theology is a rooted and nonsectarian theology of resistance and liberation, opposing it is a militant ideology of conquest and colonization, in the shape of Zionism. After a century of struggle for the liberation of their homeland, Palestinian Muslims and Christians alike—and even those who consider themselves secular—have come together in a tertiary theological liberation space that transcends their sectarian affiliations.

In the American context, sociologist Robert Bellah proposed the idea of an "American civil religion," as before him, French sociologist Émile Durkheim thought of religion as what he called "collective consciousness."[36] Today, while Bellah's idea of civil religion remains a potent sociological proposition, it has effectively lost to the vicious Evangelical Zionism that supports both the most reactionary faction of the Republican Party and the Israeli settler colony. If we were to put the ideas of Bellah and Durkheim together and recast them onto the Palestinian context, we might consider the collective consciousness of Palestinians, who wish to liberate their homeland from European conquest undergirded by Zionist ideology. Palestinians must, therefore, come together to form a unique liberation theology that transcends Christianity and Islam.

The roots of Evangelical Zionism can be traced back to the time of Bartolomé de las Casas (1484–1566), when settler-colonial Christianity was put squarely at the service of the European conquest of the "New World."[37] Palestinian liberation theology, on the other hand, is rooted in Latin American liberation theology, as best articulated by Dominican priest Gustavo Gutiérrez, among others. In my most recent work, I have extensively mapped out a post-Islamist liberation theology that is equally evident in the ecumenical project of Palestinian liberation theology, which brings Muslim and Christian Palestinians together.[38] In a future Palestinian national framework, any Islamist outfit that may exist will have to contend not just with other non-Islamist factions, but more importantly, with a deeply cultivated and nonsectarian citizenry. As such, those factions will be subject to a post-Islamist liberation theology that takes the *collective suffering* of Palestinians as its point of departure. In the form of Palestinian national liberation, Islam and Christianity have already come together against the ideology of conquest in the form of Zionism. This is not religious warfare, nor a battle of theologies. This is a struggle between a fanatical religious zealotry and a nonsectarian citizenry building the vision of a post-Zionist future.

Palestinian liberation theology is syncretic, nonsectarian, and nondenominational. It is at once Christian and Islamic, while neither entirely Christian nor entirely Islamic—it takes the moral imagination of both and pivots it toward righting the wrongs done to a people. "Here in Palestine," Isaac said in his sermon, "the Bible is weaponized against us, our very own sacred text. In our terminology in Palestine, we speak of the Empire. Here we confront the theology of the Empire—a disguise for superiority, supremacy, 'chosenness' and entitlement." This, in plain truth, pits the embracing universality of Palestinian liberation theology against the myopic and tribal Zionism fully at the service of Western imperialism. History is on the side of the brutalized—and yes, this time, "blessed are the meek, for they shall inherit the earth" (Matthew 5:5).

"Free, Free Palestine!"

For many decades, American Jews have built our political identity on a contradiction: Pursue equal citizenship here; defend group supremacy there. Now here and there are converging. In the years to come, we will have to choose.[39]

Peter Beinart, "The Great Rupture in American Jewish Life" (*The New York Times*, March 22, 2024)

Whether or not responsible and conscientious Jews will ever dismantle Zionist ideology to save their ancestral faith in line with a Jewish liberation theology still remains to be seen. There are plenty of post-Zionist and even anti-Zionist currents within Jewish communities, but not a credible critical mass to dismantle Zionism. Equally, and perhaps more important than these abundant signs of a Jewish, Christian, or Islamic liberation theology beyond their respective sectarian sentiments, there remains the prospect of a decidedly Palestinian liberation theology that includes and liberates all these entrapped world religions, including and particularly Judaism. Might we hope that one day the prophetic voices of a post-Zionist Jewish liberation theology will join a Palestinian liberation theology as a reality sui generis?

The final decoupling of "Israel" and "the West" can only happen if the hope of a Jewish liberation theology joins forces with the evident fact of a Palestinian liberation theology. To approach that possibility, we must begin with solid reality: There is no active and consistent solidarity with the Palestinian cause without a simultaneous and equally active solidarity with the memory of the Jewish Holocaust and the enduring pain of the survivors and descendants of some staggering six million Jews who were murdered during the Nazi genocide.[40] Nelson Mandela is reported to have said: "We know too well that our freedom is incomplete without the freedom of the Palestinians." We should match that wisdom by acknowledging the fact that Palestinian freedom is also incomplete without the liberation of Jews from Zionism. This is much more than a mere principled act of solidarity. Jews have been the internal Other of the West in the same way that the world at large has been made the external Others of the selfsame "West." The hatred of Jews and the hatred of Muslims are definitive to the xenophobic frenzy of the delusion that calls itself "the West." We cannot overcome that racism unless and until Jews join the entirety of the colonized world to dismantle the racist delusion of the West that has weaponized their historic sufferings for the colonial conquest of Palestine. For that to happen, we need to see the rise of a post-Zionist Jewish liberation movement in the same way that we see the rise of a post-Islamist liberation theology.

In a characteristically brilliant piece for *The New York Times*, Peter Beinart wrote:

> For the last decade or so, an ideological tremor has been unsettling American Jewish life. Since Oct. 7, it has become an earthquake. It concerns the relationship between liberalism and Zionism, two creeds that for more than half a century have defined American Jewish identity. In the years to come, American Jews will face growing pressure to choose between them.[41]

Alas, Beinart seems inattentive to the fact that precisely during that half a century of Zionism and whitewashed liberalism, Palestinian voices exposing that lie had been systematically and consistently demonized, denigrated, dismissed, and denied. Was Edward Said's eloquent voice not heard by liberal Zionists? How could anyone read or hear Said in the 1970s and 1980s and still think liberal Zionists could have it both ways? Said's seminal book *The Question of Palestine* (1979) was published half a century before Beinart wrote these words in 2024.[42] Today, the work of a scholar like Shaul Magid relies on the historical evidence of that sustained course of fissure between the prophetic voice of Judaism and the false fury of Zionism. Magid's bold and precise attempt to retrieve the exilic character of Judaism (to which I return in my conclusion) is rooted in his involvement in the counterculture movement of the 1960s. He in fact identifies his politics as "counter-Zionism."

> By "counter," I also mean an ideology that resists the ethnocentrism that in my view lies at the very heart of Zionism. Counter-Zionism, free from ideological claims and proprietary principles, free from the intoxication of power, can provide a vision of nationhood that includes (and does not simply tolerate) ethnic differences. Such a state would not be founded on the notion that "this is our land, and we will

give you a piece of it on our terms;" rather, it would be predicated on the principle that "we live on this land together on equal footing and neither party can claim ownership any more than the other."[43]

Magid's position is put in decidedly political terms. But I am pointing to the prospects of its sublimations into post-Zionist, post-Islamist, and post-Evangelical liberation theological terms. Today, Zionists have been cornered into siding with the most reactionary protofascistic forces in American and European politics. It was a delusion that Zionists could be liberal too. The nightmares of Zionism are bold, brilliant Jewish voices heard loud and clear around the globe, denouncing Zionism as a misbegotten, genocidal delusion. In the rising choirs of Jewish voices against the terror of Zionism, we are witness to the emergence of a Jewish liberation theology, with far-reaching implications for the world at large. Here are the eloquent, precise words of Naomi Klein:

> Zionism is a false idol that has betrayed every Jewish value, including the value we place on questioning—a practice embedded in the Seder with its four questions asked by the youngest child. . . .
>
> Today, this false idol justifies the bombing of every university in Gaza; the destruction of countless schools, of archives, of printing presses; the killing of

hundreds of academics, of journalists, of poets—this is what Palestinians call scholasticide, the killing of the means of education. . . .

Our Judaism is not threatened by people raising their voices in solidarity with Palestine across lines of race, ethnicity, physical ability, gender identity and generations.

Our Judaism is one of those voices and knows that in that chorus lies both our safety and our collective liberation.[44]

This is also the voice of a Palestinian liberation theology, where Jews have as much historic roots and rights as any other Palestinian—Muslim, Christian, or, Lord love them all, atheists and agnostics too.

CHAPTER 3

Poetry After Genocide

Sajjil ana Arabi ...
Write it down!
I am an Arab!
My Identity Card Number is 50,000!
I have eight children!
The ninth of them is due after the summer.
Does that trouble you![1]

Mahmoud Darwish, "*Bitaqah Huwiyyah /*
Identity Card" (1964)

In 2014, I wrote an essay dwelling on Theodor Adorno's pointed phrase: "To write poetry after Auschwitz is barbaric."[2] My concern at that point was to test the thematic limits of a German Jewish philosopher justly troubled by the Holocaust and its echoes in the case of the massacre of

Palestinians in their homeland. Did Adorno have anything to tell and teach us beyond his own immediate concerns? Recently, I have wondered how we might answer the question today.[3] I am no longer convinced that critical thinkers like Adorno, eminent in their own time and for their own immediate purposes, have anything serious to say about our world, the world outside Europe, the world at large, the world in which the destruction of Gaza and the genocide of Palestinians have not just returned to the headlines but have, in fact, radically altered our perception, reception, and encounter with our history.

The Jewish Holocaust that so troubled Adorno, as it ought to trouble us all, has now been completely cast onto the global context of other equally horrifying genocides of which Adorno and the entire Frankfurt School he iconically represented were woefully ignorant or else toward which were indifferent. In *Genocidal Empires: German Colonialism in Africa and the Third Reich* (2018), Klaus Bachmann detailed meticulously the terror the Germans had perpetrated on African people before they turned attention internally to their own people. Bachman writes:

> German colonialism belongs to the darker parts of the German past. It remains a puzzle until today. It was neither profitable for Germany, nor was it a period of which contemporary or later generations

could be proud of. Although pride was predominant in the political speeches of the day, throughout the colonial period between the Berlin Conference and World War I German officers, German bureaucrats and German soldiers looked up to the British as the more experienced, more senior colonizers, from which the Germans could learn how to effectively deal with "the natives," how to organize colonies, and how to develop them.[4]

What happened in Germany during the Holocaust was the rule, not an aberration in German imperial history. The savage treatment of Indigenous peoples and transatlantic slavery were the rule and not the exception in the course of "Western Civilization." By the same token the barbaric behavior of the US during the Vietnam War (1955–1975) was not an aberration but the rule of this settler colony. The same is true with what the Spaniards did in the Americas, the British in India, the French in Algeria, the Germans in Africa, or the Dutch in Indonesia, and so on. These were not exceptions or aberrations but the rule, a rule that is now fully displayed in what Israeli settler colonialists are doing in Gaza and the rest of Palestine. Does this mean it is barbaric to compose poetry after what Israel has done in Palestine? Is perhaps the function of poetry different in "the Rest" than it is in "the West"? Are we to follow Adorno's advice and look at Palestinian poetry before and after the Palestinian genocide as barbaric, useless, pointless, or insufficient?

Poetry Then and Now

Write it down!
I am an Arab!
I work in a quarry with my friends.
I provide for my eight children!
Their bread, clothing, and stationeries,
I carve out of stones!
No I do not beg for charities at your doors,
Nor do I humble myself at your front porch!
Does that trouble you![5]
   Mahmoud Darwish, *"Bitaqah Huwiyyah /*
Identity Card" (1964)

Let's place what Adorno says about poetry after Auschwitz in its proper European and American context—the two continents the German philosopher called home. In his essay, "Cultural Criticism and Society" (1949), where he made his famous assertion, Adorno observes that "the traditional transcendent critique of ideology is obsolete," which is to say, "there are no more ideologies in the authentic sense of false consciousness, only advertisements for the world through its duplication and the provocative lie which does not seek belief but commands silence."[6] In other words, so far as he can see the project at the epicenters of capitalist modernity, ideological tropes have hit a narrative cul-de-sac and, therefore, are incapacitated in their critique of ideology, for the European philosopher and the theorist is integral to that ideology. The insularity of that hegemonic ideology has now degenerated into varied shades of advertisements, which in turn engulf and transmute the very nature of our critical faculties. Ideology, in short, has become amorphous. But most obviously in saying so, Adorno has the European and particularly American frames of his references. How that ideological formation is systematically decomposed on the colonial ends of capitalist modernity is beyond his perspective. The world at large was not where Adorno was at, even when Adorno was writing this essay in 1949, not just historically or geographically, but morally, imaginatively, and poetically. In short, when he thought poetry after Auschwitz was barbaric, he was thinking of German or perhaps English and French poetry, where the terror of the Holocaust was most immediately felt, and certainly not poetry in other languages and cultures in Asia, Africa, or Latin America, where the brutish and murderous character of capitalism and its genocidal traces were far more evident much earlier than Auschwitz.

"Mahmoud Darwish is a literary rarity," the leading scholars and translators of the iconic Palestinian poet tell us.[7] "Critically acclaimed as one of the most important poets in the Arabic language and beloved as the voice of his people, he is an artist demanding of his work continual transformation and a living legend whose lyrics are sung by fieldworkers and schoolchildren."[8] Darwish has, in short, become synonymous with his poetry, and his poetry with his occupied and stolen homeland. But at the same time, his towering command of Arabic poetry has made him a household name in the entirety of the Arab world and, in fact, through his translations beyond. "Few poets have borne such disparately bestowed adulation, nor survived such dramatic vicissitudes of history and fate as Mahmoud Darwish; even fewer have done so while endeavoring to open new possibilities for poetry while assimilating one of the world's oldest literary traditions."[9] Such opening of horizons in a language and a poetic tradition that has deep roots in classical masterpieces is no small feat. Darwish's poetic presence, integral to his Palestinian character, has become integral to contemporary Arabic poetic and political consciousness. I read Darwish first in Persian long before I read him in Arabic or English. He was one of the poets with whom my political and poetic consciousness took shape.

As a Palestinian and an Arab poet, Darwish, however, belongs to a larger constellation of poetic consciousness. "Darwish's poetic fraternity," his translators and admirers report, "includes Federico García Lorca's *canto hondo* (deep song), Pablo Neruda's bardic epic range, Osip Mandelstam's elegiac poignancy, and Yehuda Amichai's sensitive lyric responsiveness to the contemporary history of the region. As a poet of exilic being, he resembles C. P. Cavafy, and shares with other poet-exiles of the past century a certain understanding of the exilic condition of literary art."[10] This description is fine, but it is not the complete constellation of poets to which Darwish belonged, nor, indeed, does it reveal the degree to which Darwish was at home in that constellation and, therefore, his "exilic" disposition overcompensated by redefining the world in which a Palestinian poet would be best understood. Like Faiz Ahmad Faiz in Urdu, Ahmad Shamlou in Persian, Nâzım Hikmet in Turkish, Vladimir Mayakovsky in Russian, Federico García Lorca in Spanish, or Langston Hughes in English, Mahmoud Darwish, too, had cast the political predicament of his homeland into a universal diction of our world. A world that, in its entirety, from one end to another, in languages and cultures, critical and creative thinking, is completely and utterly terra incognita to Adorno and his entire generation of German and European philosophers—myopic, tribal, and provincial as they have been. German, Italian, or English poetry might be barbaric after Auschwitz, for those are the languages in which the horrors of the Holocaust happened and were perpetrated—but certainly not in Arabic or any number of other languages adjacent to it, where the predicament of

Palestinians is part of a history of genocidal colonialism, perpetrated long before Europeans turned to other Europeans.

Darwish was a master of classical Arabic poetics and prosody. But obviously there is more to Palestinian poetry than just Darwish. "Perhaps no other Palestinian popular poet garnered the fame and popularity of Nuh Ibrahim."[11] Why was Nuh Ibrahim (1913–1938) important—even before the establishment of the Israeli settler colony, before the Nakba? "Unlike other Palestinian poets from the twentieth century who wrote in Modern Standard Arabic [*fusha*] and published in newspapers and journals, Nuh Ibrahim recited and sang his poems in the colloquial dialect and was the poet of the common people, expressing what they experienced and felt."[12] Ibrahim is today remembered as a folk poet, a singer, a composer, and a freedom fighter during the British mandate. The rebellious character of Nuh Ibrahim, the folkloric power of his verses, and the timing of his short life place him at the crosscurrents of British colonialism and the rise of the Israeli settler colony. In that moment, in the moment of Nuh Ibrahim's poetry, the entire course of European colonialism comes through to institutionalize itself in the formation of the Zionist state—and, with it, the poetic disposition of rebellion charged against that legacy.

Adorno's Time and Ours

Write it down!
I am an Arab!
I am a name with a surname!
Quite patient in a land where everything
Is quick to anger!
My deep roots
Reach deeply before time began,
Before the opening of epochs,
Before the cypress and olive trees,
And before the green grass began to grow ...[13]
  Mahmoud Darwish, *"Bitaqah Huwiyyah /*
  Identity Card" (1964)

A key point Adorno makes in "Cultural Criticism and Society" is the paradoxical position of the persona of the (European or "Western") critic from the person of their whereabouts in the society they inhabit. This is how Adorno formulates the larger issue:

> Cultural criticism finds itself faced with the final stage of the dialectic of culture and barbarism. To write poetry after Auschwitz is barbaric. And this corrodes even the knowledge of why it has become impossible to write poetry today. Absolute reification, which

presupposed intellectual progress as one of its elements, is now preparing to absorb the mind entirely. Critical intelligence cannot be equal to this challenge as long as it confines itself to self-satisfied contemplation.[14]

In other words, the European critics themselves are implicated; they are the bearers of the reified ideology, as indeed Adorno himself was thoroughly implicated in the ideology of the West. And he never figured it out! How can one criticize what one cannot see, for one is implicated in it? There is no distance between the European knowing subject and the colonized knowable world that was to be de-reified, demystified, defetishized, and critically deconstructed. Rudyard Kipling's barbaric poetry in defense of British colonial savagery was the supreme sign of civilization. But when that reification boomeranged into the West itself—then poetry became barbaric. One cannot perform heart or brain surgery on oneself—Adorno finds out. The problem with Adorno in that diagnosis is the problem with all other European philosophers, except he openly mourns the fact that the epistemic bifurcation between the European knowing subject and the world laid bare at the disposal of their commanding authority has finally vanished in Europe itself. For the rest of the world, for the colonized, this is a moment of liberation, for we have ceased to be knowable to our European masters and their knowing subjects, our tormentors, the thieves, the officer class, the priestly class, who came and plundered and preached, and went home and wrote anthropological monographs on us and taught them in their universities. Adorno thinks he has discovered a reified world that deeply troubles him, but that world was the byproduct of barbaric colonial enterprise, which he never bothered to even fathom.

Adorno works his way toward that critical conclusion from the very outset of the essay:

> To anyone in the habit of thinking with his ears, the words "cultural criticism" (*Kulturkritik*) must have an offensive ring, not merely because, like "automobile," they are pieced together from Latin and Greek. The words recall a flagrant contradiction. The cultural critic is not happy with civilization, to which alone he owes his discontent. He speaks as if he represented either unadulterated nature or a higher historical stage. Yet he is necessarily of the same essence as that to which he fancies himself superior.[15]

To Adorno's German ears the fusion of Greek and Latin is quite offensive, but more urgently, "the cultural critic," *Kulturkritik* or otherwise, is a self-deluding person who has no ground of their own on which to stand and distinguish the truth from the falsehood. The theoretical issue, however, assumes urgent critical agency for Adorno when it comes to the Holocaust, for the genocide of European Jews and other atrocities of fascism, as he and Horkheimer would argue in *Dialectic of Enlightenment* (1947) was not despite but because of the instrumental reason at the heart of Enlightenment modernity. Adorno is, therefore, facing a dead-end where the emancipatory power of the Kantian *sapere aude* has, in fact, ended up in the German concentration camps. The supreme stage of civilization for Adorno has, therefore, ended up being entirely barbaric. So, with Auschwitz, the world ended, society and culture ended, civilization had yielded to barbarism. What could poetry possibly have left to say? That kind of philosophical nihilism and epistemic cul-de-sac is perfectly understandable and categorically European, for the entirety of the world that was decidedly placed outside the domain of European Enlightenment had never entertained that illusion to then be disillusioned, as Walter Mignolo, among others, has argued and demonstrated in *The Darker Side of Western Modernity: Global Futures, Decolonial Options* (2011).

Now consider this: I come from a history, a civilization, and a literary tradition that, we believe, in the aftermath of the Mongol invasion of the thirteenth century, was saved and recrafted precisely by poets like Rumi and Sa'di and later Hafez—among scores of others. Poetry is needed precisely when barbarism takes over. But when we read the history of our literary traditions, we were never implicated in the illusion of any partition between our knowing subject and the amorphous world we tried to decipher. That violent arrogance was exclusive to European Enlightenment modernity, which Adorno both criticized and yet was deeply implicated in. When we engage with our literary traditions, we believe what the world needs, during and in the aftermath of barbarism of the sort Europe witnessed in Auschwitz, is the poetic intuition of transcendence it had lost as it lost its soul when colonizing the globe. Adorno thinks poetry is barbaric both because the cultural critic is integral to that which they criticize and also because Auschwitz was so uniquely barbaric. He says so because he never saw Asians, Africans, or Latin American victims of European colonial savagery as capable of their own civilization. Therefore, European poetry after European genocides in Asia, Africa, and Latin America was perfectly fine, but not after Auschwitz. We need to think about the Jewish Holocaust and the Palestinian genocide together and wonder what sort of poetry is possible.

Here we need not necessarily refer to other literary traditions around the world of which Adorno was ignorant, but in fact resort to a very odd place indeed, namely Adorno's philosophical archnemesis Heidegger in an essay he published a decade before Adorno's text, titled "What Are Poets For?" (1936). In this essay, Heidegger articulates, in his own roundabout way, the significance of the work of poets: "'And what are poets for in a destitute time?' asks Hölderlin's elegy

'Bread and Wine.' We hardly understand the question today. How, then, shall we grasp the answer that Hölderlin gives?"[16] Heidegger insists on beginning with the word "time," which for him in this context "means the era to which we ourselves still belong." Heidegger crafts his own mythic version of what that time means for Hölderlin, yet, of course, we can gather the sense of doom and gloom that defines Heidegger's reading of Hölderlin. What matters is how Heidegger opts to end with the Austrian poet Rainer Maria Rilke: "If Rilke is a 'poet in a destitute time' then only his poetry answers the question to what end he is a poet, whither his song is bound, where the poet belongs in the destiny of the world's night. That destiny decides what remains fateful within this poetry."[17] So are we then, by analogy between Hölderlin and Rilke, where Nuh Ibrahim and Mahmoud Darwish stand in relation to Palestine, time and space? How is that "world's night" different from the image Darwish invokes in his "deep roots":

> Reach deeply before time began,
> Before the opening of epochs,
> Before the cypress and olive trees,
> And before the green grass began to grow . . . ?[18]

From Adorno to Fanon, Pontecorvo, and Said

> *I am a name without a surname!*
> *Write it down!*
> *I am an Arab!*
> *My Address:*
> *I am from an isolated, forgotten village*
> *Its streets are nameless...*
> *Does that trouble you?*[19]
>
> **Mahmoud Darwish**, "*Bitaqah Huwiyyah /*
> Identity Card" (1964)

One should not, nor can we afford, to be fatalistic. We must seek the light through the depth of this terror and darkness. As I write these words in mid-July 2024, the highly respected peer-reviewed British medical journal *The Lancet* reports that some "186,000 or even more" Palestinians have been slaughtered by genocidal Zionists in Gaza.[20] This is reported to be 7.9 percent of the total population of Gaza.[21] To think of the power and necessity of poetry after the enormity of such horrors in Gaza beyond the myopic reach of Adorno or any other European's self-indulgent gloom, we need, as always, to open up our horizons beyond the Eurocentric imagination.

Let us consider the towering Italian filmmaker Gillo Pontecorvo (1919–2006) and his iconic film *The Battle of Algiers /*

La battaglia di Algeri (1966). Pontecorvo was born in Pisa, Italy, in 1919 to a prominent and well-to-do Jewish family. At a very young age, in 1938, he left for Paris, escaping rampant antisemitism, and by 1941 he had joined the Italian Communist Party and went to northern Italy to join the anti-fascist partisans. By 1943, he had become a leader of the Resistance in Milan. By 1956, when the Soviet Union crushed the Hungarian Revolution, Pontecorvo left the Communist Party. By then, he had become a major filmmaker and was about to make his iconic film, *The Battle of Algiers*, in 1966. He continued to make other films, but none surpassed the significance of *The Battle of Algiers*.[22]

Frantz Fanon (1925–1961) came to Algeria from Martinique, just before Pontecorvo came to the same place from Italy. Both of them were critically drawn to the brutality of the French colonization of the North African nation. Fanon had published his *Black Skin, White Masks* in 1956, a *Dying Colonialism* in 1959, and his signature text, *The Wretched of the Earth*, in 1961. Although Pontecorvo may or may not have known of Fanon's work, the thematic link between Fanon and Pontecorvo is self-evident.[23] Banned in France for years, *The Battle of Algiers* eventually gained a reputation for inspiring urban guerrilla warfare by the Black Panthers, the Provisional Irish Republican Army, the Jammu Kashmir Liberation Front, and the Red Army Faction. The Pentagon screened the film in 2003, just before the US invasion of Iraq, showing how it could be used for other ends.[24]

Why should Pontecorvo, an Italian Jewish filmmaker, travel all the way to the Arab country of Algeria in North Africa and make a film about the Algerian anticolonial uprisings? For years I have taught this film and shared with my students the idea that the events of the Warsaw Ghetto Uprising (1943), which occurred when Pontecorvo was a twenty-four-year-old anti-fascist partisan, had a profound and enduring impact on the visual registers of *The Battle of Algiers*.[25] When we compare the black-and-white pictures of the Warsaw Ghetto Uprising with the shots of *The Battle of Algiers*, we see remarkable similarities, which is perhaps the reason Pontecorvo decided to create his film in black-and-white newsreel style. When, in 1966, at the age of forty-seven, Pontecorvo made *The Battle of Algiers*, the heroic memories of the Warsaw Ghetto Uprising against German Nazi savageries were very much on his mind. Pontecorvo simply translated that event into his take on the Algerian uprising against French colonialism. Equally important is to locate the making of *The Battle of Algiers* in the aftermath of Pontecorvo's break with the Italian Communist Party in 1956 after the Soviet intervention to suppress the Hungarian uprising. Pontecorvo is drawn to Algeria as an expanded domain of liberation politics. Years later, Edward Said made a documentary on Pontecorvo and *The Battle of Algiers* based on a conversation with the Italian director in 1988.[26] What we see in that documentary is a Palestinian critical thinker pushing Pontecorvo to expand upon his lifetime interest in anticolonial struggles. In one frame, we see Frantz Fanon (Afro-Caribbean), Gillo Pontecorvo (Jewish Italian), and Edward Said (Christian Palestinian) sharing a transnational commitment to liberation entirely overcoming their incidental biographical locations. That in and of itself was and remains a liberation poetics beyond the geographical imagination of Adorno or any other European philosopher of his rank.

Poetry after genocide is not barbarism. Quite to the contrary: It is the supreme sign of ennobling civilization, the sign of life and liberty of a people to fight against barbarism. The shock of the Holocaust for Adorno was so paralyzing, and rightly so, that there was nothing uplifting or insightful left to be said. For Adorno as a European and a German at the receiving end of Nazi savagery, his words remain perfectly legitimate. The context for Adorno, though, was not just the condemnation of the Holocaust but the condemnation of the Holocaust as the final stage of capitalist modernity, when cultural critics themselves had become part and parcel of the problem—as indeed Adorno himself had become implicated in the myth of the West. When we step out of that European context, the world opens itself up to poets like Aimé Césaire. And, of course, Mahmoud Darwish. Pontecorvo's *Battle of Algiers* was true poetry after the Holocaust, a movie created in active collaboration with Algerian revolutionaries and in the memory of the Warsaw Ghetto Uprising. Adorno, the Frankfurt School, and Critical Theory will remain a touchstone landmark in the history of European philosophical legacy, with much to teach the world, including, and perhaps particularly, where it so glaringly failed to learn anything from the world outside of Europe.

CHAPTER 4

Philosophy After Savagery

The Negroes of Africa have by nature no feeling that rises above the ridiculous. Mr. Hume challenges anyone to adduce a single example where a Negro has demonstrated talents, and asserts that among the hundreds of thousands of blacks who have been transported elsewhere from their countries, although very many of them have been set free, nevertheless not a single one has ever been found who has accomplished something great in art or science or shown any other praiseworthy quality, while among the whites there are always those who rise up from the lowest rabble and through extraordinary gifts earn respect in the world. So essential is the difference between these two human kinds, and it seems to be just as great with regard to the capacities

of mind as it is with respect to color. . . . The blacks are very vain, but in the Negro's way, and so talkative that they must be driven apart from each other by blows.[1]
Immanuel Kant, *Observations on the Feeling of the Beautiful and Sublime* (1764)

We believe that amidst all the conflicting views being expressed, there are some principles that should not be disputed. They are the basis of a rightly understood solidarity with Israel and Jews in Germany.[2]
Nicole Deitelhoff, Klaus Günther, Rainer Forst, and Jürgen Habermas, "Principles of Solidarity. A Statement" (2023)

The lines above are quoted from a statement published soon after Israel started carrying out its latest phase of Palestinian genocide in Gaza, a genocide that had begun decades ago and culminated in what Palestinians rightly call their Nakba/Catastrophe of 1948. That Nakba is ongoing. The statement in question was cosigned by the senior German philosopher Jürgen Habermas, and published in mid-November, when Israel's vicious mass murder of Palestinians was still underway.[3] Up to that point, I had pondered this deeply rooted bigotry in European philosophy for more than a decade, but had never thought of it rearing its head with such astounding vulgarity while Palestinians were being killed in their tens of thousands. I published a short piece in response to the statement, proposing a link between the documented affiliation of Martin Heidegger with Nazism and Jürgen Habermas's Zionism, where the suffering of the manufactured Other, internal or external to Europe, was of no philosophical (moral or political) significance. My larger point in this short essay was to argue that we, as non-Europeans, simply do not exist in the European philosophical imagination, from Kant to Hegel to Levinas and the rest of their pedigree.[4] We simply lack ontological reality except as a sort of metaphysical menace, a racialized noise, that must be quieted, conquered, and pacified. This is the reason why the murder of tens of thousands of Palestinians does not quite register in their so-called moral imagination. Between me and the German philosopher lie the mass graves of an entire homeland.

There is a habitual practice among older and younger generations of European philosophers—they almost exclusively cite European thinkers when using the term and the institution of "Philosophy," thereby laying an exclusive claim on the word and what it means. The practice frequently traces the origin of contemporary European philosophy to the Greeks, entirely disregarding the fact that these Greek sources had an entirely different gestation and resonance in the Eastern Mediterranean domains of Islamic and Jewish thoughts. The questions I have pondered in my work are not only historical, but also categorical and rhetorical. What I have wondered over many decades is whether people around the globe in Asia, Africa, or Latin America had a claim to this word, "Philosophy," and what it means to have such a claim.

The problem that has preoccupied me throughout these studies is not those Europeans who are included in this self-centering practice of Philosophy, but the more obvious question: whether thinkers outside Europe had anything resembling philosophy that a person might cite and consider. My concern was and remains twofold—the epistemic foregrounding of excluding non-Europeans from the domain of thinking and the ontological possibility of any mode of philosophical thinking outside the European imaginary. The predicament is as follows: If Europeans are the only people who can philosophize, then other people by virtue of not philosophizing are not human.

What I have strived to do over decades of work, before Habermas delivered his coup de grâce, has been to overcome and dismiss the false universal claims of "Western philosophy" and to expose its irredeemably racist foundations. Western philosophy is tribal and white supremacist, disregarding the totality of our humanity. Understanding the vicious legacy of "the West" and its philosophy is also a prerequisite for a clearer critique of that which has sold itself to the world as "Western liberalism." Following that line of thinking, we can see how Israeli Prime Minister Benjamin Netanyahu is not an anomaly but in fact the logical product of the Israeli political system (just as Trump is in the US). The blind spots of the West, of Western Philosophy, and, above all, of Western liberalism were finally exposed in the course of the Palestinian genocide.

For the longest time, the world has been hoodwinked and cast in the false shadow of "European moral philosophy." I have adamantly opposed the idea that philosophers like Habermas were being hypocritical in disregarding Palestinians as human beings. In fact, he is perfectly consistent and logical within his imagination, just as Kant and Hegel and Heidegger before Habermas did not bat an eye, dismissing entire swaths of humanity. More than ever before, it has now become evident that Eurocentric philosophy has always been a tribal affair, faking universality by virtue of the brutish military might of the West, and not by virtue of any epistemic credibility or rational argument. Dismantling the false universal claims of Western Philosophy is a necessary step toward allowing for the ruins of Gaza to emerge as the metaphysical foundation of a radically different way of thinking of the world philosophically. The racist legacy of European philosophy reflected in Habermas's views has no place in that emerging philosophical imaginary of the world at large, except as the extension of those dismounted statues of slaveholders in European or American city squares. Those statues ought to be taken down and placed in some distant museum of human miseries: This is how we must from now on read "Western philosophy."

As I write these words in July 2024, the International Court of Justice has officially declared Israel's presence in Palestinian territory as illegal and that Israeli practices in these occupied territories amount to annexation.[5] In response, Israeli leaders accused the court of "antisemitism."[6] In other words, the European murder of six million Jews has been weaponized to silence, frighten, and scandalize any decent human being, any court of law, that dares to point to the criminal thuggeries of genocidal Zionism. The delusions of Western philosophy undergird the material violence of Zionism.

The Phenomenology of Hegel's Racist Spirit

Indeed, Father Labat reports that a Negro carpenter, whom he reproached for haughty treatment of his wives, replied: You whites are real fools, for first you concede so much to your wives, and then you complain when they drive you crazy. There might be something here worth considering, except for the fact that this scoundrel was completely black from head to foot, a distinct proof that what he said was stupid.[7]

Immanuel Kant, *Observations on the Feeling of the Beautiful and Sublime* (1764)

Habermas's Zionism, as indeed Heidegger's Nazism, are rooted in a much deeper and longer European philosophical racism. The vulgar racism of Kant's philosophy, or the philosophy of many other European thinkers in his rank, should not be read as personal. Rather, it is definitive to their philosophical system. A significant body of scholarship has now produced persuasive evidence of the unabashed racism of leading European philosophers, from John Locke (1632–1704) to David Hume (1711–1776) to Immanuel Kant (1724–1804) to G. W. F. Hegel (1770–1831) and others. This racism is not incidental to their philosophical imagination and projects and, therefore, cannot be excused or sidestepped.

In "Philosophy's Systemic Racism," (2020) Avram Alpert, a research fellow at the New Institute in Hamburg and the author of *A Partial Enlightenment: What Modern Literature and Buddhism Can Teach Us About Living Well Without Perfection* (2021) demonstrates how racism seeped into the very structures of Hegel and Rousseau's philosophy.[8] Central to this racism is the phenomenon of European colonialism, which European philosophers followed closely: "If we look to two of Hegel's immediate predecessors in the dialectical method—Jean-Jacques Rousseau (1712–78) and Friedrich Schiller (1759–1805)," Alpert writes, "we can see how the method itself was influenced by colonial history as much as by Plato or magnetism. Rousseau had a profound influence on Hegel. And he, like Hegel, was a voracious reader of accounts from colonial ethnographers and missionaries."[9] We cannot, therefore, remove the reality of colonialism from the aloof and august domain of their philosophical speculations. European philosophy has been so thoroughly whitewashed and sanitized of its historical contexts that even suggesting a context for the writings of any serious European philosopher sounds sacrilegious. Yet it is imperative to strip European philosophy of its false self-universalization, which has come at the expense of domesticating, nativizing, ethnizing other ways of thinking.

Many contemporary European philosophers and scholars exert their most earnest efforts to rescue an older generation of philosophers from their rampant and textually evident racism. But as with the case of Heidegger and as evident in his recently discovered *Black Notebooks* (2014), antisemitism was not incidental to Heidegger's philosophy but in fact definitive to it.[10] As the extensive scholarship of Richard Wolin, among others, but especially his seminal study, *The Politics of Being* (2016) shows, Heidegger's critique of modernity was rooted in his antidemocratic and antisemitic thoughts.[11] In a crucial book, *Heidegger: The Introduction of Nazism into Philosophy in Light of the Unpublished Seminars of 1933–1935* (2011), Emmanuel Faye has identified critical and unabashed antisemitic tropes and sentiments in Heidegger's philosophical thinking. Similarly, the racist thoughts of major philosophers like Hegel and Kant were rooted in their extensive facilities with European colonialism. That racism, however, is not limited to the seminal works of these philosophers but extends right into the curricular spectrum of contemporary departments of philosophy. We need to be as scrupulous and determined exposing the racism of Hegel, Kant, and Levinas as scholars have rightly been revealing Heidegger's Nazism. Institutionally, we need to demand curricular changes in departments of philosophy, rescuing them from their entrapment within European tribalism.

In a probing essay, "Exploring the Metaphysics of Hegel's Racism: The Teleology of the 'Concept' and the Taxonomy of Races" (2022), Daniel James and Franz Knappik have exposed "Hegel's hierarchical theory of race as an application of his general views about the metaphysics of classification and explanation."[12] This is no tangential or personal racism. This is racism as the building block of a philosophical system. In their judgment, "Hegel's views about a hierarchical and necessary division of humankind into races are an application of this model to the case of human diversity, motivated by explanatory considerations and subject to confirmation bias."[13] As responsible scholars, James and Knappik do their best to "'save' Hegelian philosophy from its racist baggage."[14] But they rightly put "save" in quotation marks. The alternative to saving Hegel's philosophy from its inerasable racism is not discarding or demonizing Hegel. Quite to the contrary, my argument is that we must reread these philosophers anew in light of their racism. The alternative is, therefore, to historicize, locate, and thus deuniversalize European philosophy, to cut it down to its proper size, as one among many other forms of philosophical dispositions, neither best nor worst— one among many others, with its blindness and insights. We therefore need to create an "anthropology" of European philosophy, as it were. European anthropologists have turned the entirety of humanity outside of Europe into a laboratory of their racialized and colonial gaze. Decolonizing philosophy departments requires this necessary stage of an anthropology of European philosophy.

You would be surprised (if not aghast) to observe the mental and verbal gymnastics some scholars stage in vain to save Hegel from the racist foundations of his philosophy. In "Race and Racism in Hegel—An Analysis" (2006), Sandra Bonetto acknowledges how "many of Hegel's critics have argued that the philosopher provided a basis for modern racism and established a role for race in history by correlating a hierarchy of civilizations to a hierarchy of races, notably in the *Encyclopedia* and the *History of Philosophy*." But she proceeds to hold: "Hegel's comments on race and racial diversity" do not make him a racist.[15] It makes absolutely no difference if Hegel was personally a racist person or not. In fact, it is entirely flawed to abandon the philosophical system Hegel has left behind and fall into the wild-goose chase of finding out whether Hegel was or was not personally racist. It is imperative for the argument never to become ad hominem. This gist of Sandra Bonetto's argument is as follows:

> Negative value judgements concerning various cultures or cultural practices, however ill-informed and arrogant we might find them today, do not automatically amount to racism. For racism, as far as I understand it, is motivated by an unreasonable or irrational hatred and/or fear of the "other" *qua* "other," coupled with the desire either to dominate, discriminate against or exclude that "other" (e.g. by favoring the establishment of laws or social practices to this end). In other words, racism is different from ethnocentrism.[16]

As a philosopher, Hegel was indeed rationalizing that hatred, so it would not be an "irrational hatred." Hegel did not have an irrational hatred of non-Europeans. He sought to offer a solidly rational argument for that diabolical hatred. But Bonetto does not seem to see the political (colonial) foundations of that rationalization of racism. Hegel did not do the *dominating*, for he was just a philosopher not a colonial officer. But he certainly systematized the groundwork for the *discriminating* that German and other European colonizers were doing around the world. Hegel's tribalism, or "ethnocentrism," was the very foundation of his philosophy. This does not make him, or else exempt him, from being personally racist. The issue is not ad hominem, the issue is institutional, systematic, philosophical. Heidegger had an affair with Hannah Arendt, one of his Jewish students.[17] This has nothing to do with the systematic and terrible antisemitism definitive to his philosophy.

In an insightful essay, "Racism and Rationality in Hegel's Philosophy of Subjective Spirit" (1992), Darrel Moellendorf demonstrates how "the eurocentrism of Hegel's philosophy of history is well known. Hegel's reputation has not benefited from many of the claims in the *Philosophy of History*; such as the one that African history, having no development, has contributed nothing to world history."[18] Moellendorf is fully aware of the excuses that some European scholars continue to make for Hegel's racism. "An obvious apology for Hegel's position," he writes,

> would be to claim that he simply did not know of the struggles and achievements of Africans, that this knowledge is the result of later historiography. The difficulty with this position is that Hegel most surely was aware of both the resistance on the part of slaves and of their achievements. He demonstrates knowledge of the massive slave uprising in Haiti, inspired by the same principles of the French revolution

which he held so dear: "They [Blacks] cannot be said to be ineducable, for not only have they occasionally received Christianity with the greatest thankfulness and spoke movingly of the freedom they have gained from it after prolonged spiritual servitude, but in Haiti they have even formed a state on Christian principles."[19]

According to Hegel, Africans, or any other people, can only become civilized to the degree and so far as they abandoned their own cultures and convert to Christianity, founding a state according to Christian principles. We are all by now aware of the "Kill the Indian, Save the Man" doctrine of Christian boarding schools in the US and Canada and the sustained history of violence with which they sought to pacify those who were resisting their thieveries.[20] One must not confuse and conflate this reactionary and colonizing European and Eurocentric Christianity with the Christianity at the heart of Latin American liberation theology that has a vastly different and radically emancipatory reading of the faith.

In "The Dark Side of Hegel's Theory of Modernity: Race and the Other" (2019), Jong Seok Na of Yonsei University demonstrates how "Hegel's theory of race in particular, his philosophy of spirit in general, provides the justification of a colonial racism or a cultural racism. While Hegel's theory undoubtedly contained racist elements, still unanswered is whether racism is inherently at odds with the basic principles of his philosophy of spirit."[21] Na proceeds to hold that "racism is fundamentally incompatible with the basic principles of Hegel's philosophy of spirit, notwithstanding its undeniably racist elements."[22] And yet he goes through a sustained and judicious examination of Hegel's philosophical racism to come to this conclusion:

> If our quest is to open a new forum for discussing Hegelian philosophy with regard to searching for a genuine universalism beyond [a] European universalism, the starting point must be the recognition of non-Western societies as equal partners of intercultural dialogues. In order to overcome the limits of Hegel's philosophy of spirit, Frantz Fanon's last sentence in *The Wretched of the Earth* should be again reminded: "For Europe, for ourselves, and for humanity, comrades, we must turn over a new leaf, we must work out new concepts, and try to set afoot a new man."[23]

This, indeed, is a noble idea. However, if we need to correct the racist lenses of Hegel with the critical humanism of Fanon, then we have taken but one step in the right direction. The false universalism of European philosophy that has been achieved through murderous colonial practices will have to be deuniversalized and provincialized before that "genuine universalism" is anywhere in sight.

The critical apparatus necessary to dissect Hegel's racist philosophy still has a very long way to go. In "Where Did Hegel Go Wrong on Race?" (2024) Michael O. Hardimon tells us that "Hegel's treatment of race begins systematically in the *Philosophy of Subjective Spirit* and that he went wrong philosophically in the use of the biological category of race. This is basically correct but requires precisification." He then moves on to consider "why Hegel's category of race is not unambiguously biological. Race's biological status can be problematized from the standpoint of contemporary biology and from the standpoint of Hegel's system."[24] The problem with this line of argument is the habitual and unexamined primacy given to salvaging Hegel. The task at hand is not to save Hegel but to unpack the foundations of his philosophical system and to bring European provincialism into the larger context of other domains of critical thinking.

In a key intervention, Robert Bernasconi, a leading professor of philosophy and African American studies, puts it bluntly: "The unwillingness of philosophers generally to confront, for example, the failure of Locke and Kant to oppose the African slave trade does not arise out of a healthy refusal to engage in tabloid philosophy, but represents both a moral and a philosophical shortcoming."[25] This is, of course, putting it very generously. Let us read Bernasconi closer:

Take Locke, first. It is true that Locke scholars for a number of years have recognized the need to address the question of his leading role in the administration of British colonial activities and his investment in the slave trade through the Royal African Company, as well as the Company of Merchant Adventurers, who operated in the Bahamas, but the consideration of these topics is still largely the preserve of historians and political theorists, as if they raised no philosophical questions.[26]

They do raise philosophical questions, of course. Bernasconi then proceeds to identify three tasks facing philosophers today (not just intellectual historians, as he clarifies): "These three tasks—identifying the problematic statements of these thinkers that are prima facie racist, locating them in the context of their works and the broader historical context, and establishing their sources—are basic tasks that intellectual historians would perform as a matter of course, although they involve scholarly and historical skills that philosophy graduate programs, for the most part, do not spend much effort in developing among their students."[27] The last point is precisely where the problem lies: Professional philosophers and scholars of philosophy are not prepared to ask these uncomfortable questions—for if they did, the whole enterprise might collapse. What this leads to, of course, is an unexamined commitment to keep the word "philosophy" contained to existing Eurocentric departments, disciplines, professional academic journals, and institutions of philosophical scholarship. Bernasconi underlines the key critical issue: "So who is the real Kant? The real Kant apparently is not the historical Kant but, rather, the author only of his central philosophical principles. The real Kant is defined not by texts so much as by select ideas that contemporary Kantianism finds valuable."[28] Western philosophy is where ideas are disembodied, texts are dehistoricized, speculations are falsely universalized, all at the full expense of turning other philosophical projects into "ethnophilosophy." This disciplinary malady has some very serious and dangerous political consequences of the sort we see in Heidegger's Nazism or Habermas's Zionism.

Truth and Irreconciliation

Spatially central, the ego cogito constituted the periphery and asked itself, along with Fernández de Oviedo, "Are the Amerindians human beings?" that is, Are they Europeans, and therefore rational animals? The theoretical response was of little importance. We are still suffering from the practical response. The Amerindians were suited to forced labor; if not irrational, then at least they were brutish, wild, underdeveloped, uncultured—because they did not have the culture of the center.[29]

Enrique Dussel, *Philosophy of Liberation* (1980)

Works such as Victor Farias's *Heidegger and Nazism* (1987/1991) were bold and brilliant in dismantling the taboo of thinking politically about European philosophy. We need nothing less precise in exposing the colonial and racist roots of European philosophy. We can speculate about the philosophical, ontological, and epistemic foregrounding of that philosophy and wonder whether it is incidental, or ad hominem, or whether these discussions amount to "tabloid philosophy," but what ultimately matters for the world at large is the categorical inability to fathom a Palestinian as a human being. The conclusion is not to stop reading European philosophy, but to start rereading European philosophy "anthropologically," as ethnographic evidence of a racist tendency that could only speculate philosophically about the world by excluding vast swaths of humanity from it, placing these vast swaths of humanity at the receiving end of its "reason," as they were at the receiving end of their guns and fighter jets.

There are honest and noble attempts to try to read the eminent French philosopher Emmanuel Levinas as related to "postcolonial thoughts," seeking to justify or explain away when he says: "I often say, although it is a dangerous thing to say publicly, that humanity consists of the Bible and the Greek. All the rest can be translated: all the rest—all the exotic—is dance." Or another gem: "When I speak of Europe, I think about the gathering of humanity. Only in the European sense can the world be gathered together. . . . In this sense Buddhism can be said just as well in Greek." Or this shining pearl: "I always say—but under my breath—that the Bible and the Greeks present the only serious issue in human life; everything else is dancing. . . . There is no racism intended."[30] Indeed, no racism at all. I do wonder why the eminent French philosopher keeps saying he is not supposed to say these things publicly, just to think them quietly to himself. But that rumination is less relevant than the phrase "humanity consists of the Bible and the Greek." What of the Mesopotamian context of the Bible? The rest of us, the rest of our humanity, outside the European appropriation of the Greeks exclusively for themselves, are left wondering what to do with ourselves. So if a Palestinian does not fit Levinas's expectations, then are they not human?

We need to keep clearly in mind the kinds of cruelty that this legacy of European philosophy and its most illustrious figures have enabled to be perpetrated with impunity. "Since the beginning of the Israeli bombardment and ground invasion in Gaza," *The New York Times* reports, citing several Palestinian rights groups, including the Palestinian Prisoners' Commission, "the Israeli Army arrested hundreds of Palestinians in a barbaric and unprecedented manner and has published pictures and videos showing the inhumane treatment of detainees."[31] This is the historical context of Habermas's defense of Israel as it perpetrates a genocide, and the context in which we read Levinas telling us if we do not read the Greeks and the Bible the way he, as a European, reads them, then we are not human. The same report continues: "So far, Israel has concealed the fate of detainees from Gaza, has not disclosed their numbers, and prevented lawyers and the Red Cross from visiting detainees."[32] This is not a humanitarian crisis. This is a philosophical calamity. Israel is treating Palestinians, as their leaders say, as "inhuman animals." In another even more precise report by CNN, they wrote of "a facility where doctors sometimes amputated prisoners' limbs due to injuries sustained from constant handcuffing; of medical procedures sometimes performed by underqualified medics earning it a reputation for being 'a paradise for interns;' and where the air is filled with the smell of neglected wounds left to rot."[33] As a "human animal" myself, as an Iranian with a lifetime commitment to the Palestinian cause, I too smell that rot while reading Habermas, Levinas, Kant, or Hegel. The same report continues: "They stripped them down of anything that resembles human beings." When I read that phrase, I think of the entire history of European philosophy and what it represents.

Reading Reality After Gaza

Distant thinkers, those who had a perspective of the center from the periphery, those who had to define themselves in the presence of an already established image of the human person and in the presence of uncivilized fellow humans, the newcomers, the ones who hope because they are always outside, these are the ones who have a clear mind for pondering reality. They have nothing to hide. How could they hide domination if they undergo it? How would their philosophy be an ideological ontology if their praxis is one of liberation from the center they are opposing? Philosophical intelligence is never so truthful, clean, and precise as when it starts from oppression and does not have to defend any privileges, because it has none.[34]

Enrique Dussel, *Philosophy of Liberation* (1980)

After the unbridled savagery in Gaza, it is not only European philosophy that reaches its ignoble ends. We need equally to think of the modes of knowledge production about Gaza itself, about Palestine, as the simulacrum of the world outside the purview of the discredited Eurocentric imagination. We no longer need to worry about the critique of Orientalism. We need to think of how to produce knowledge about Gaza and Palestine and the rest of the world.

We need to reverse the anthropological gaze, to produce an anthropology of Zionism and Western Philosophy. Paramount is changing whom we think of as our interlocutor, of whom we are talking to. If the language of Orientalism was Orientalists talking to colonial officers, then in the prose I have identified as post-Orientalist, we opt to change the interlocutor altogether. We were and we are talking to each other in the Global South. We are talking to and with disenfranchised communities in the Global North. After Gaza, we have a radically different task ahead. We are no longer talking to the fiction of "the West," explaining ourselves, for the illusion of the West has lost all credibility. I was not, and I am not, talking to Habermas or to European supporters of Israel when I underline the irredeemable racism of their philosophy. I do not wish to convince them of anything. I was and I am talking to Palestinians, to Arabs, to Muslims, to people in Asia, Africa, Latin America, and to vast swaths of people in the Global North who are conversant with us.

What sort of epistemology might inform our reading of reality after what is happening in Gaza, when the metaphor of the West has reached a dead end, and the liberated prospects of "the Rest" have arisen? From the classical mode of knowledge production known as Orientalism, we moved on to Area Studies, and from there to the rise of purposeful and useful think tanks at the service of imperial projects, and from

PHILOSOPHY AFTER SAVAGERY

there to the current condition of "Security Studies." In all these varied gestations, knowledge was at the service of power. From Edward Said's *Orientalism* (1978) to my *Post-Orientalism* (2009), from Said's defiant humanism to the current rise of post-humanism in the works of critical thinkers like Rosi Braidotti's *Posthuman Knowledge* (2019), global fields of knowledge are in a state of flux. When Israeli officials call Palestinians "human animals," they are ignorant of the fact that they are marking the geological age of the Anthropocene as Eurocentric colonial savageries against the planet earth. Political paralysis after the Palestinian genocide must be a prelude toward an epistemic liberation. Taking stock of the colonial, postcolonial, and decolonial fields, where Edward Said, Gayatri Spivak, and Homi Bhabha have become a cliché North American triumvirate, the horrors of the Palestinian genocide give purposeful direction to these disciplines of knowledge production beyond anything we have seen before. The guiding principle, in short, of thinking philosophy after savagery, of how we get to know and read the realities we face after what is happening in Gaza, of how to do philosophy after the Palestinian genocide, must remain steadfast to overcoming such paralyzing reports:

> GENEVA (19 February 2024) – UN experts today expressed alarm over credible allegations of egregious human rights violations to which Palestinian

women and girls continue to be subjected in the Gaza Strip and the West Bank.

Palestinian women and girls have reportedly been arbitrarily executed in Gaza, often together with family members, including their children, according to information received. "We are shocked by reports of the deliberate targeting and extrajudicial killing of Palestinian women and children in places where they sought refuge, or while fleeing. Some of them were reportedly holding white pieces of cloth when they were killed by the Israeli army or affiliated forces," the experts said.[35]

CHAPTER 5

The Garrison State Versus the Palestinian Camp

Dr. Mark Perlmutter, an orthopedic surgeon from North Carolina, and vice president of the International College of Surgeons, volunteered in Gaza from the end of April through the first half of May. Asked to describe what he witnessed in Gaza, Dr. Perlmutter replied, "All of the disasters I've seen, combined—40 mission trips, 30 years, Ground Zero, earthquakes, all of that combined—doesn't equal the level of carnage that I saw against civilians in just my first week in Gaza."

And the civilian casualties, he said, are almost exclusively children. "I've never seen that before," he said. "I've seen more incinerated children than I've ever seen in my entire life, combined. I've seen more shredded

> *children in just the first week . . . missing body parts, being crushed by buildings, the greatest majority, or bomb explosions, the next greatest majority. We've taken shrapnel as big as my thumb out of eight-year-olds. And then there's sniper bullets. I have children that were shot twice."*
>
> *"I have two children that I have photographs of that were shot so perfectly in the chest, I couldn't put my stethoscope over their heart more accurately, and directly on the side of the head, in the same child. No toddler gets shot twice by mistake by the 'world's best sniper.' And they're dead-center shots."*[1]
>
> "Children of Gaza," by **Tracy Smith**,
> CBS News, *Sunday Morning* (July 21, 2024)

In the course of the Palestinian genocide, two glaring realities have emerged and faced each other: Israel is a heavily militarized garrison state, and Palestine is a constellation of refugee camps at the mercy of Israeli systemic violence since the Nakba. Israel has taken the form of a total state with no legitimate nation, facing Palestinians as a fragmented nation with no legitimate state. This interface is both factual and symbolic. It is factual for Palestinians and the violence they face. It is symbolic within a larger global context, where the total state on the model of Israel has become the norm and the fragmentation of nations into camps, their correlated consequences.

THE GARRISON STATE VERSUS THE PALESTINIAN CAMP 105

In American sociology and political science, the term "garrison state" is understood as a state apparatus that is dominated by radically militarized conceptions of polity, economy, and society. The constitution of an enemy—formerly the Soviet Union and now Russia and China for the US, or the Arabs and Palestinians for Israel—is definitive to the formation of a garrison state. This characteristic of the garrison state is directly rooted in the Nazi political theorist Carl Schmitt's seminal book *The Concept of the Political* (1932). The military budget of a garrison state like the US or Israel is astronomical, disproportionately higher than any other budget for social services. In Israel, most inhabitants of the garrison state are old, new, or soon-to-be soldiers. Although the idea of the garrison state is American in its origin, the corresponding Canadian idea of "garrison mentality" is equally applicable to Israel. Zionists have a fundamental fear of their environment, very much on the model that the term was first coined by Canadian literary critic Northrop Frye in his *Literary History of Canada* (1965). Both Canada and Israel, as European settler colonies, have an enduring fear of the natives in their countries and thus run away into their fortified garrisons, or "villas," away from the surrounding jungle.[2]

The idea of "the camp," meanwhile, has received particular attention from the Italian philosopher Giorgio Agamben, who considers it the central theme of the entire project of European modernity. Agamben's idea begins with the proposition that life has been debased to the biopolitics of bare life, leading to the denial of inalienable rights. This proposition is predicated on the distinction he makes between "bare life" (*zoē*) and a "qualified life" (*bios*). From here, he concludes and proposes "the Camp as the *Nomos* of the Modern," where the state of exception on the site of the camp becomes the rule. The inhumane conditions of life in the camp places the location and inhabitants of the camp outside the fold of humanity, mortality, polity. This state of exception is, in fact, the state of modernity as Europe has crafted and violently universalized it—though this last point is beyond Agamben's frame of reference.

Much of the literature on the "garrison state" and "the camp" treat their subject matter independently of the other. In this chapter, I wish to present them as intertwined, with Israel as the paramount example of the garrison state and the entire life of Palestinians, wherever they live, inside or outside of refugee camps, as a state of exception made unexceptional. Here, Palestine stands for both its own historical dispossession under the pointed gun of Zionism and for the fate of our humanity at large at the mercy of capitalist modernity militarized as colonialism. The problem with both the theorization of the garrison state and the camp is the missing link of the colonial. The one concept, theorized by American political scientist Harold D. Lasswell, and the other concept, theorized by the Italian philosopher Giorgio Agamben, and, of course, both concepts expanded on by other scholars, have had little to no conception of the colonial condition. That colonial condition is the locus classicus of both the garrison state and the camp. Dr. Mark Perlmutter's words at the beginning of this chapter shows us why the savagery unleashed on Palestine is where we must see the interface between the garrison state par excellence and the camp writ large.

The Israeli Garrison State

Last month, speaking in Washington, D.C., other American doctors echoed Dr. Perlmutter's calls for help. Dr. Feroze Sidhwa said, "We've described it as a catastrophe, a nightmare, a hell on Earth. It's all of these, and worse."

Dr. Zena Saleh said, "We didn't even have hand sanitizer or alcohol or soap most of the time."

"While we're there, we're listening to, you know, 'Aid is getting in. We're taking care of civilians. They're not being targeted,'" said Dr. Adam Hamawy. "And yet, we're witnessing a completely different story." . . .

One Chicago-based doctor told us, "I thought these kids were in the wrong place at the wrong time, like, sadly, some of the kids we treat in Chicago. But after the third or fourth time, I realized it was intentional; bullets were being put in these kids on purpose."

> *Dr. Perlmutter noted that he saw, for dozens of miles, 18-wheelers parked bumper-to-bumper, their engines off or idling, outside of Gaza. "Food or health care could not get in," he said. [I] asked, "How many kids are in danger of starvation in Gaza?" "All of them," he replied. "Absolutely all of them."*[3]
>
> "Children of Gaza," by **Tracy Smith**, CBS News, *Sunday Morning* (July 21, 2024)

What is a garrison state? In a pioneering essay from 1941, published in the midst of World War II, American political scientist Harold D. Lasswell inaugurated a crucial idea that would remain definitive to generations of scholarship. "The purpose of this article," he wrote, "is to consider the possibility that we are moving toward a world of 'garrison states'—a world in which the specialists on violence are the most powerful group in society. From this point of view the trend of our time is away from the dominance of the specialist on bargaining, who is the businessman, and toward the supremacy of the soldier."[4] President Dwight D. Eisenhower's farewell address (1961), warning against the formation of what he termed a "military-industrial complex," perfectly corroborated and exemplified the premonitory insights of Lasswell. Of all people, or perhaps particularly because he was a military man himself, Eisenhower stated: "This conjunction of an immense military establishment and a large arms industry is new in the American experience.... Yet we must not fail to comprehend its grave implications.... In the councils of government, we must guard against the acquisition of unwarranted influence, whether sought or unsought, by the military-industrial complex. The potential for the disastrous rise of misplaced power exists and will persist."[5]

Lasswell fully realized the social and political dynamics at work in the formation of a garrison state. "There will be an energetic struggle," he wrote, "to incorporate young and old into the destiny and mission of the state. It is probable that one form of this symbolic adjustment will be the abolition of 'the unemployed.' This stigmatizing symbol will be obsolete in the garrison state."[6] In other words, the state metastasizes to absorb the nation in its totality and civil society in its varied forms of public sphere. The state becomes totalitarian, while seemingly still "democratic." Astonishing perspicacity on the part of Lasswell to have seen through the totalitarian tendencies of the garrison state, smack in the middle of a presumption of "democracy." "In the garrison state," he wrote, "all organized social activity will be governmentalized; hence, the role of independent associations will disappear, with the exception of secret societies ... Government will be centralized, though devolution may be practiced in order to mitigate 'bureaucratism.'"[7] "Governmentalized" is another term for the formation of the total state, and thus pure violence, right at the heart of what believes itself to be a "democracy." Lasswell was, in fact, diagnosing the formation of Germany during its Nazi era in the 1930s when he wrote this essay early in 1940s. He did not, therefore, hesitate from calling the garrison state "dictatorial":

> We have sketched some of the methods at the disposal of the ruling élites of the garrison state—the management of propaganda, violence, goods, practices. Let us consider the picture from a slightly different standpoint. How will various kinds of influence be distributed in the state? Power will be highly concentrated, as in any dictatorial regime. We have already suggested that there will be a strong tendency toward equalizing the distribution of safety throughout the community (that is, negative safety, the socialization of threat in modern war).[8]

In a much later study, *In the Shadow of the Garrison State: America's Anti-Statism and Its Cold War Grand Strategy* (2000), Aaron L. Friedberg, a professor of politics and international affairs at Princeton University, sought to suggest a safeguard against that totalitarian tendency of the garrison state in the US. He formulates his argument on the assumption of the US having been built on "the suspicion of state power."[9] Because of this presumed feature of US politics, Friedberg believes post–Cold War anxieties did not lead to the US becoming a garrison state. This study was premature, as a frightful garrison state did emerge in the aftermath of September 11, 2001. Today, reactionary elements in US politics are doing precisely what Lasswell thought they would, turning the country into a militaristic totalitarian nightmare.[10] The agents of this degeneration are precisely the reactionaries who oppose government so much they want to take it over.

A far more accurate reading of the garrison state appears in Milton J. Esman's "Toward the American Garrison State" (2007):

> A garrison state is a polity in which military priorities and internal security have first claim on their nation's resources. The more the imperium is threatened overseas, the tighter the garrison state at home.
>
> In the wake of 9/11, the War on Terror became the supreme priority of the U.S. government. Foreign threats to the security of the homeland were now a clear and frightening danger to the American public. Civilians would be even more at risk than the military. President Bush announced that the United States would oppose terrorists everywhere, as well as governments that harbor and support them. The United States would not relent in its War on Terror until terrorists had been defeated everywhere.[11]

Meanwhile, outside the US, where the idea was first theorized, Israel has received much scholarly attention as a garrison state. Dwight J. Simpson, professor of international relations at San Francisco State University, was a pioneering scholar in this field. In a study published soon after the 1967 War, "Israel: A Garrison State" (1970), he begins with a jubilant celebration of the Israeli state apparatus:

> It has been more than two years since Israel administered a military defeat to her Arab neighbors, principally Egypt, Syria and Jordan. The "desert blitzkrieg," which lasted only six days in June of 1967, revealed beyond any doubt or discussion that the Israeli war machine was incomparably superior in all respects to the pathetically inept Arab armies. Indeed, so overwhelming was the Arab military defeat that it was commonly predicted in the summer of 1967 that it would take the Arab states several years simply to replace their military equipment, most of which was destroyed or captured by the Israelis.[12]

That the Israeli military was enabled, empowered, and heavily weaponized by the US and Europe is, of course, nowhere in sight in this study. But still Israel here stands as the "garrison state" erected and empowered by the West, protecting its regional and global interests on the ground. Later in the study, Simpson's prose cools off to realize the nature of this military machine:

> All these events have been very painful for Israel to absorb. First, they have been costly in terms of lives lost and property destroyed. The total of Israelis killed or wounded during 1969 has been very high and, proportionate to Israel's population, has nearly equaled the casualties suffered by United States forces in Vietnam. Second, they have more or less frozen Israel into the posture of an embattled garrison state, with all the negative social, economic and political consequences that this implies. Due to continuing Arab pressure from the various Arab government forces or from the Al-Fatah units, it has not been possible for Israel to return since 1967 to anything resembling peacetime conditions.[13]

Israel, since its very inception, has been an active garrison state, created as such by Europe and kept afloat as a military base by the US. As such, Simpson's remark on "returning" to peaceful conditions is misguided, as that peaceful time never existed.

In yet another study, *Garrison State: Israel's Role in U.S. Global Strategy* (1985), Steve Goldfield has examined Israel in considerable detail as a garrison state in its relations with the

US.[14] The main argument of the study here, by now quite clear if not cliché, is the serious role of the US in building Israeli military foundations as a garrison state and how Israel's role in the region is defined in terms of US interests. Definitive to this relationship is the role of the US in Israel acquiring nuclear capabilities. In a pioneering study, *The Samson Option: Israel's Nuclear Arsenal and American Foreign Policy* (1991), American investigative journalist Seymour M. Hersh detailed the history of the Israeli quest for the atom bomb since the 1950s and the crucial role of successive US administrations, including the spying role of Jonathan Jay Pollard, in helping Israel achieve its nuclear capacities.[15] Today, Israel is one of the most lethal nuclear powers in the world, definitive to its status as a garrison state.

The link between garrison states, colonialism, and pure violence is written into the very fabric of Israel, as first a European and now an American settler-colonial project. In this respect, the model of many states in the region, not just Israel, becomes ISIS, the Islamic State of Iraq and Syria, the notorious terrorist organization that devastated the region in the immediate aftermath of the collapse of Iraq under US conquest and civil war in Syria. Citizens as citizens no longer have even a categorical presence under these circumstances, where they become naked lives, where ISIS forms the amorphous shape of a "total state" sustained via "pure violence." In this sense, the garrison state is the return of the barely repressed origin of all states, for which all innocent civilians have become what the Italian philosopher Giorgio Agamben has called "homo sacer" (the accursed person, the bare life). Unable to protect their citizens, states lose their basis of legitimacy and become, like ISIS, a "state" without a nation supporting it. Israel, as a garrison state, effectively mirrors this model.[16]

The garrison state belies the end of the institution of the nation-state. The Weberian conceptualization of the "state" as an entity with a monopoly over violence that requires a certain degree of moral legitimacy is no longer operative, for now garrison states wield absolute and brutal power over many populations. As ruling states become killing machines targeting nations, this pure violence is unleashed onto a bare life, a life shorn of its biographical dignity, stripped of civic protections and dispossessed of its rights.[17]

The Muselmann: From the Jewish to the Palestinian Camp

The untestifiable, that to which no one has borne witness, has a name. In the jargon of the camp, it is der Muselmann, *literally "the Muslim."*[18]

Giorgio Agamben, *Remnants of Auschwitz: The Witness and the Archive* (1999)

Why were emaciated Jews referred to as *Muselmänner* in German concentration camps? On the surface, it does not quite make sense unless the two feared and loathed figures in the German, or European, imagination are conflated: a dying Jew, a dying Muslim.

Over the last few decades, the Italian philosopher Giorgio Agamben has put forward the compelling proposition that modern states are rooted in the concentration camps they run and that their sovereignty is rooted in the systematic destruction of human life these camps best represent. Despite the fact that Agamben scarcely thinks or writes about the Israeli settler colony and its Palestinian concentration camps, he has inadvertently been theorizing that bare truth on the ground. As always, when we read a European philosopher, we must read and decipher them from the vantage point of their own blind spots. I read Agamben's *Remnants of Auschwitz* (1999), and I am always baffled that the central figure of "the Muselmann" is never traced back to what it actually means, a Muslim, rather than to what the Germans made of it in the concentration camps.

On a rare occasion, Agamben has written about Palestinians. In a chapter titled "Beyond Human Rights" in *Means Without End: Notes on Politics* (1996), he writes that he saw on the news a group of Palestinians stranded in what he called a no-man's-land.[19] From here, Agamben begins to theorize these homeless Palestinians into his schemata of the camp:

These men certainly constitute, according to Hannah Arendt's suggestion, "the vanguard of their people." But that is not necessarily or not merely in the sense that they might form the originary nucleus of a future national state, or in the sense that they might solve the Palestinian question in a way just as insufficient as the way in which Israel has solved the Jewish question. Rather, the no-man's-land in which they are refugees has already started from this very moment to act back onto the territory of the state of Israel by perforating it and altering it in such a way that the image of that snowy mountain has become more internal to it than any other region of Eretz Israel. Only in a world in which the spaces of states have been thus perforated and topologically deformed and in which the citizen has been able to recognize the refugee that he or she is—only in such a world is the political survival of humankind today thinkable.[20]

On this rare but still important occasion, Agamben clearly suggests that the formation of Palestinian refugee camps is definitive to the modernity of the Israeli settler colony, except the distinguished Italian philosopher skips over the term "settler colonial." We need to place that term right back where it belongs. To do so, a clear understanding of the term "Muselmann," as used in the Nazi concentration camps is crucial. But first read what Agamben says carefully. When Agamben writes that this no-man's-land has become internal to the state of Israel, he has already marked the formation of the state of Israel as a coda of European colonial modernity. So it is not "from this very moment" in 1993 when the world (and Agamben) got a glimpse of Palestinian refugees, but it is from the moment in 1948, when the state of Israel was first created by the West, and from 1917, when the Balfour Declaration first officialized the settler colony. The key connecting factor in the European racist imagination for this simultaneous formation of both the Israeli garrison state and the Palestinian camps is the term "Muselmann," as German Nazi mass murderers used it on behalf of European antisemites and Islamophobes combined.

Back to the main question: Why call a dying Jew a Muslim? In his *Remnants of Auschwitz*, Agamben examines a number of possible explanations. This was not the only term the German concentration camp guards used for dying Jews. Agamben relates the following from Wolfgang Sofsky's *The Order of Terror: The Concentration Camp*:

> The expression was in common use especially in Auschwitz, from where it spread to other camps as well. . . . In Majdanek, the word was unknown. The living dead there were termed "donkeys"; in Dachau they were "cretins," in Stutthof "cripples," in Mau-

thausen "swimmers," in Neuengamme "camels," in Buchenwald "tired sheikhs," and in the women's camp known as Ravensbrück, Muselweiber (female Muslims) or "trinkets."[21]

Now consider the terms "Muselmann," "tired sheikhs," "camels," and "female Muslims" together and you can sense the Muslim hatred of Germans exposing itself in terms of their hatred of the Jews they were actively engaged in mass murdering. Their two common objects of blind hatred—the Jew and the Muslim—have here collapsed onto each other. "Muselmann" is, therefore, conceptually homonymic: The term means two different (but now made interrelated) things at one and the same time. Agamben's speculations about the term "Muselmann" are important here:

> The most likely explanation of the term can be found in the literal meaning of the Arabic word Muslim: the one who submits unconditionally to the will of God. It is this meaning that lies at the origin of the legends concerning Islam's supposed fatalism, legends which are found in European culture starting with the Middle Ages (this deprecatory sense of the term is present in European languages, particularly in Italian)....
>
> There are other, less convincing explanations. One example appears in the *Encyclopedia Judaica*

under the entry Muselmann: "Used mainly at Auschwitz, the term appears to derive from the typical attitude of certain deportees, that is, staying crouched on the ground, legs bent in Oriental fashion, faces rigid as masks." Another explanation is suggested by Marsalek, who associates "the typical movements of *Muselmänner*, the swaying motions of the upper part of the body, with Islamic prayer rituals."[22]

This is perhaps a mini encyclopedia of European ignorance, Islamophobia, and antisemitism all wrapped up in an attempt to unpack the word "Muselmann," but in fact loading it with more racist dimensions. Agamben reveals the fact that these "deprecatory" aspects of the word "Muslim" are palpably present and evident in European languages, "particularly in Italian." Agamben then concludes aptly: "In any case, it is certain that, with a kind of ferocious irony, the Jews knew that they would not die at Auschwitz as Jews."[23] This is true. But it could also be read in reverse, namely not just that a Jew is dying a Muslim but also that a Muslim is dying in absentia a Jew, and, therefore, the two detested metaphors have come together in their moment of factual and metaphoric annihilation. In the figure of the emaciated "Muselmann," the German word for "the Muslim," the dying Jew becomes the dying Muslim, and vice versa, as both become Orientals, one internal to Europe and the other external to it. Limited within his own European imagination, Agamben, could not overcome that racialized topography and see what, in fact, happens to the emaciated Jew when called a Muslim. Conflating them, the internal and external Others of Europe, allows the German to become fully "European" at the moment when Germany was waging an existential war against Europe.

In the figure of the Muselmann, the genocidal urges of colonial modernity become evident at the moment when Germans were slaughtering their own internal Others long after they had done so in Africa with their external Others—a fact that never even occurs to Agamben. In German concentration camps, Nazis were foreshadowing Zionists turning Palestine in its entirety into a constellation of refugee camps. Agamben therefore, was in fact theorizing Palestine as the colonial site, as "the nomos" of the modern, without even noticing it, for while he rightly paid attention to Auschwitz, Bergen-Belsen, Börgermoor, Buchenwald, Dachau, he gave no notice to Yarmouk, Rafah, Khan Yunes, Ain al-Hilweh, Burj el-Barajneh, Qalandia, Jenin, Sabra, Shatila, Darra. This is the epistemic limitation of a European philosopher at the moment of their most radical speculations and insights. All Agamben had to do was to take a quick look at the history of his own country, to consider what Mussolini was doing in Libya during the Libyan genocide of 1929 and 1934. Those Italian concentration camps for Libyans would have also made for an excellent study of camps as the nomos of colonial modernity. The word that Libyans themselves use for the Libyan genocide is Shar/Evil—this is a good place to start reflecting on the nomos of colonial modernity.

Palestinian Camps as the Site of (Colonial) Modernity

The so-called Muselmann, as the camp language termed the prisoner who was giving up and was given up by his comrades, no longer had room in his consciousness for the contrasts good or bad, noble or base, intellectual or unintellectual. He was a staggering corpse, a bundle of physical functions in its last convulsions. As hard as it may be for us to do so, we must exclude him from our considerations.[24]
Jean Améry quote in Giorgio Agamben, *Remnants of Auschwitz: The Witness and the Archive* (1999)

While Agamben was writing the site of Nazi concentration camps into the nucleus of his theorization of modernity, he was inadvertently also historicizing the site of the Palestinian refugee camps as the site of the colonial shadow of the self-same modernity. We should, therefore, read the colonial into Agamben when he was theorizing the darker side and the cul-de-sac of European capitalist modernity. Agamben's central argument in his seminal work *Homo Sacer: Sovereign Power and Bare Life* (1995) is solid: "Today it is not the city but rather the camp that is the fundamental biopolitical paradigm of the West"—this is the defining moment of modernity for "there is no return from the camps to classical politics."[25] Yet again, the correction is obvious: Long before the camp became "the fundamental biopolitical paradigm of the West," the selfsame "West" perpetrated it on "the Rest," on the colonial world. Today, Israel is staging that homicidal paradigm on Palestine. The colonial blind spots of European philosophers are worthy of a whole equestrian statue unto itself.

"What happened in the camps," writes Agamben, "so exceeds the juridical concept of crime that the specific juridico-political structure in which those events took place is often simply omitted from consideration." That structure is assumed and presumed to be limited to "the Western context." The "Western" colonial conquest of the globe extended that juridical "context" and superimposed it as the rule of the jungle around the world. More precisely, Agamben writes: "The camp is merely the place in which the most absolute *conditio inhumana* that has ever existed on earth was realized: this is what counts in the last analysis, for the victims as for those who come after."[26] Of course, with all due respect to the eminent Italian philosopher, "the most absolute *conditio inhumana* that has ever existed on earth was realized" also when Germans and other Europeans, including Italians, traveled the world and turned civilizations they could not fathom into camps. When the Belgians were slaughtering the Congolese, or the Germans were mass murdering people in Namibia, or the French in Algeria, or the British in India, ad nauseam, were these conditions not "the most absolute *conditio inhumana* that has ever existed on earth"?

For Agamben, the camp is the space of exception definitive to the rule:

> The paradoxical status of the camp as a space of exception must be considered. The camp is a piece of land placed outside the normal juridical order, but it is nevertheless not simply an external space. What is excluded in the camp is, according to the etymological sense of the term "exception" (*ex-capere*), *taken outside*, included through its own exclusion. But what is first of all taken into the juridical order is the state of exception itself. Insofar as the state of exception is "willed," it inaugurates a new juridico-political paradigm in which the norm becomes indistinguishable from the exception. . . . *The camp is a hybrid of law and fact in which the two terms have become indistinguishable.*[27]

I have traveled through Palestinian refugee camps in occupied Palestine, Lebanon, and Syria. When you walk through Sabra and Shatila in Lebanon, for example, or Yarmouk in Syria, or Tulkarem in the West Bank, the camps are both inside and outside the Lebanese, Syrian, and occupied Palestinian urban landscapes. They are more than a piece of land; they are Palestine in quotation marks. Palestinian refugee camps are indexical, citational, referential. They point back to a homeland that Zionists have stolen from Palestinians, forcing them into internal or external exile. Gaza is the very definition of "exception" as "ex-capere": A constellation of refugee concentration camps Israel has created in the very heart of the landscape they have stolen. Their exception has become normative. From a Palestinian perspective, what Agamben says makes perfect sense: *"The camp is the space that is opened when the state of exception begins to become the rule.* In the camp, the state of exception, which was essentially a temporary suspension of the rule of law on the basis of a factual state of danger, is now given a permanent spatial arrangement, which as such nevertheless remains outside the normal order."[28] That is the textbook condition of Palestinians inside and outside of Palestine, even before the creation of Israel. "In 1936," we know, "Palestinian Arabs launched a large-scale uprising against the British and their support for Zionist settler-colonialism, known as the Arab Revolt. The British authorities crushed the revolt, which lasted until 1939, violently; they destroyed at least 2,000 Palestinian homes, put 9,000 Palestinians in concentration camps and subjected them to violent interrogation, including torture, and deported 200 Palestinian nationalist leaders."[29] Poignant is Agamben's articulation that "the bare life into which the camp's inhabitants were transformed is not, however, an extrapolitical, natural fact that law must limit itself to confirming or recognizing. It is, rather, a threshold in which law constantly passes over into fact and fact into law, and in which the two planes become indistinguishable."[30] That law that has become fact for Palestinians is the law of barbarism of European colonial conquest.

It is impossible to exaggerate the significance of Agamben's articulation of the camp as the telos of European (colonial) modernity—except for the unfortunate fact that, for him, the concept of "the colonial" is almost entirely alien. "In this light, the birth of the camp in our time appears as an event that decisively signals the political space of modernity itself," Agamben writes, to which we must add "colonial modernity," so that what follows makes perfect sense:

> It is produced at the point at which the political system of the modern nation-state, which was founded on the functional nexus between a determinate localization (land) and a determinate order (the State) and mediated by automatic rules for the inscription of life (birth or the nation), enters into a lasting crisis, and the State decides to assume directly the care of the nations' biological life as one of its proper tasks. . . . The camp is the fourth, inseparable element

that has now added itself to—and so broken—the old trinity composed of the state, the nation (birth), and land.[31]

If we recall that the birth of European democratic modernity was coterminous with Europe's colonial age of conquest, then that telos was very much globally predetermined—brutally evident in Asia, Africa, and Latin America before it boomeranged in the German concentration camps. Today, the birth of Palestine as a "question" rather than a nation-state marks precisely the birth of Palestine as a constellation of refugee camps. The *land* was stolen from Palestinians, the *state* stealing the land was a European settler colony garrison state that rules over Palestinians with cruelty, the *rules* for the inscription of life were dictated to Palestinians in draconian terms, and the *camps* as the fourth inseparable element are precisely where generations of Palestinians are born and raised, before being killed by the Israeli military. Today, in Gaza and elsewhere, Palestine is turned into a "humanitarian crisis." While actively arming Israel, the US and UK feign to care for the human misery they have caused by dropping food on Gaza. With the same logic, they also speak of a "two-state solution" and even create a faux, nominal Palestinian state, in name and not in reality—where there can never be any territorial integrity or sovereignty. In this ideal model, Palestinians will self-colonize and self-police under Israeli military domination. By normalizing relations with all its neighbors, Israel is hoping to succeed in consolidating and stabilizing itself as a legitimate state, overcoming its settler-colonial roots just as Australia, the US, Canada, or New Zealand have done. Where Native Americans now live in reservations, so will the Palestinians. Palestinians might be allowed their own flag, an airline, and perhaps even a film festival and a national museum. This would all be designed to liquidate the Palestinian cause and pacify global solidarity, for that solidarity is rooted in the common misery the West has caused around the globe. Staring all such delusions in the eye is the fact of the constellation of camps from one end of Palestine to the other, where capitalist modernity is unable to confront its colonial consequences.

The Israeli Garrison State and the Palestinian Camps

I remember that while we were going down the stairs leading to the baths, they had us accompanied by a group of Muselmänner, as we later called them— mummy-men, the living dead. They made them go down the stairs with us only to show them to us, as if to say, "you'll become like them."[32]

A. Carpi quoted in Giorgio Agamben, *Remnants of Auschwitz: The Witness and the Archive* (1999)

Palestinian scholars have, of course, been fully aware of the crucial distinctions between their lived experiences of camps and Agamben's theorization of them. In "The Palestinian States of Exception and Agamben" (2009), Nurhan Abujidi complicates Agamben's perspective from a Palestinian point of view. His main argument is as follows:

> The State of Exception for [Agamben] is where an absolute use of power is performed by the sovereign against the victim who has no agency of resistance or rights as all laws are suspended and all notions are confused. . . . However, it can be stated that there is a Palestinian State of Exception, but the Exception takes different forms and operates with different dynamics. The Palestinian States of Exception entail all aspects of life—not only the juridical and legal—creating multilevels of Exception that perpetually destroys and regenerates itself in an extreme form.[33]

What becomes evident through such readings of Agamben is the modus operandi of Israel as a military base, in its originary formation, and garrison state. But the larger context of refugee camps as the nomos of capitalist modernity today has more compelling registers, allowing us to link the fate of Palestinians to the planetary disposition of dispossession. According to the UN, by May 2024, more than 120 million people have been forcibly displaced worldwide. Various factors are involved in these statistics: political persecution, military conflicts, endemic violence, or human rights violations. This total number includes: 43.4 million refugees, 63.3 million internally displaced people, 6.9 million asylum seekers, and 5.8 million people in need of international protection.[34] In *Managing the Undesirables: Refugee Camps and Humanitarian Government* (2010), Michel Agier, director of studies at the Institut de Recherche pour le Developpement and the Ecole des Hautes Etudes en Sciences Sociales, has brought to attention the crucial issue of refugees, asylum seekers, and the internally displaced in a different way.[35] These human beings are actively depoliticized, desubjected, and turned into objects of humanitarian crisis, which is itself a mode of totalitarian control and bare life. These are the "Shudras" and the "Dalits" of the planet, as it were, the wretched of the earth, the subaltern, the undesirables. In short, what Agamben wished to diagnose in the German concentration camps has a far more global implication beyond his European imagination.

In "Palestinian Refugees in Lebanon: Is the Camp a Space of Exception?" (2014), Leonardo Schiocchet has raised a number of significant issues when comparing Agamben and Agier in their readings of the camp: "Is a refugee camp indeed a space of exception? Should we understand the refugee camps in their symbolic and practical continuity or discontinuity to the urban space? Should we consider the camp as having the same properties of the 'city' in Agier's sense?"[36] The significance of these questions lies in their comparative consideration of the status of refugees as bare life, bereft of their civil (not human) rights, atomized, and at the mercy of aid organizations. That state of exception has become the rule for Palestinians. Even if inside Israel Palestinians are still treated as "enemy combatants," aliens, all as real or potential "terrorists." Schiocchet's comparison locates the status of the Palestinian refugees in the larger context of global refugees generated by predatory capitalism, which links the specific case of Palestinian defiance to the larger predicament of refugees' denial of agency. What Agamben quotes as the condition of "the Muselmann" in German concentration camps was and remains a premonition of the world at large:

> The SS man was walking slowly, looking at the Muslim who was coming toward him. We looked to the left, to see what would happen. Dragging his wooden clogs, the dull-witted and aimless creature ended up bumping right into the SS officer, who yelled at him and gave him a lashing on the head. The Muslim stood still, without realizing what had happened. When he received a second and then, a third lashing because he had forgotten to take off his cap, he began to do it on himself, as he had dysentery. When the SS man saw the black, stinking liquid begin to cover

his clogs, he went crazy. He hurled himself on top of the Muslim and began kicking his stomach with all his strength. Even after the poor thing had fallen into his own excrement, the SS man kept beating his head and chest. The Muslim didn't defend himself. With the first kick, he folded in two, and after a few more he was dead.[37]

CHAPTER 6

Palestine Beyond Borders

I write at a moment of great anguish for the world, including for many of our colleagues. Once again, we are seeing a genocide unfolding before our eyes, and the Organization that we serve appears powerless to stop it. As someone who has investigated human rights in Palestine since the 1980s, lived in Gaza as a UN human rights advisor in the 1990s, and carried out several human rights missions to the country before and since, this is deeply personal to me.

I also worked in these halls through the genocides against the Tutsis, Bosnian Muslims, the Yazidi, and the Rohingya. In each case, when the dust settled on the horrors that had been perpetrated against defenseless civilian populations, it became painfully clear that we had failed in our duty to meet the imperatives of prevention of mass atrocities, of protection of the vulnerable, and of accountability for perpetrators. And so it has been with successive waves of murder and persecution against the Palestinians throughout the entire life of the UN.[1]

From the resignation letter of **Craig Mokhiber**, director of the New York Office of the United Nations High Commissioner for Human Rights (October 28, 2023)

To resist the mutation of the Palestinian cause into a humanitarian crisis and, thereafter, the liquidation of the Palestinian national liberation movement, the cause must be solidly wedded to similar struggles around the globe for justice. The only way Palestine will remain a powerful anticolonial force is to wed its moral authority and political project for justice with similar uprisings around the globe. Jews, Christians, Muslims, agnostics, and atheists alike are today united in their collective outrage against genocidal Zionism on full display in Palestine. Predicated on that solidarity, Palestine has become the moral and imaginative premise of a radically different liberation metaphysics, irreducible to any sectarian denomination. The Palestinian national liberation struggle is now far beyond the concern of Arab or the so-called Third World countries. It is a global cry for freedom. The moral imperative of Palestine has surpassed the delusion of the West and today reaches beyond all borders.

Palestine today is at the epicenter of a radically different conception of the world—a fragile and endangered world that has overcome all its fictional frontiers and mythologies of power and politics. Soon after American imperial ideologue Samuel Huntington (1927–2008) came up with his notorious concept of the "clash of civilizations" (1992–1993), I wrote an essay on the historical flaws, ideological foregrounding, and deliberate geopolitical ruse in civilizational thinking.[2] In "For Last Time: Civilizations" (2001), I pointed out how Huntington's thesis was, in fact, entirely racist, meant primarily for domestic consumption but cast in global terms.[3] A quarter of a century after my essay, some European historians seem to have finally woken up and smelled the roses. In *How the World Made the West: A 4,000 Year History* (2024), Josephine Quinn has caught up with the whole premise of "civilizational thinking," questioning how the illusion of the West was invented. She attempts to locate the Babylonian, Assyrian, Phoenician, Indian, and Arabic, in addition to Greek and Roman, roots of this concoction, opting for a give-and-take reading of history that is late but still fine. Her point of contention is perfectly obvious: Non-Western civilizations made the West possible. She questions the idea of the West as a unique "miracle." But, in doing so, she ends up further reifying and fetishizing the idea of the West rather than seeing it for its recent invention in the course of European colonial modernity as the ideological banner of globalized capitalism.[4]

The world order that Samuel Huntington thought had just been defined in contested civilizational terms is now being systematically brutalized by Israel. Israel is the colonial extension of the logic of capital that had invented the idea of the West as its chief ideological mantra. As I write these words in early August 2024, Israel is bombing countries on several fronts. From an Al Jazeera report:

> According to an analysis of data from the Armed Conflict Location and Event Data Project (ACLED), Israel is responsible for 17,081 incidents of air/drone strikes, shelling/missile attacks, remote explosives and property destruction, in five countries—Lebanon, Syria, Yemen, Iran and the occupied Palestinian territories—since October 7.
>
> The majority of attacks have been on Palestinian territory, specifically the Gaza Strip, with 10,389 incidents accounting for more than 60 percent of total attacks.
>
> Israel conducted 6,544 number of attacks on Lebanon (38 percent), followed by Syria with 144 incidents recorded.[5]

From South Africa to Ireland, people with conscience have come to echo their defiant voices. At the same time, Israel, as the pointed arrow of "Western" imperial and colonial power, has inflicted violence on Armageddon scale. Never in our recent history have "the West and the Rest" stood so boldly against each other, to the point that we are now completely within the domain of a different, decidedly "post-Western" global configuration of power and resistance.

Empires, Colonies, Nations Beyond Borders

As a human rights lawyer with more than three decades of experience in the field, I know well that the concept of genocide has often been subject to political abuse. But the current wholesale slaughter of the Palestinian people, rooted in an ethno-nationalist settler colonial ideology, in continuation of decades of their systematic persecution and purging, based entirely upon their status as Arabs, and coupled with explicit statements of intent by leaders in the Israeli government and military, leaves no room for doubt or debate. In Gaza, civilian homes, schools, churches, mosques, and medical institutions are wantonly attacked as thousands of civilians are massacred. In the West Bank, including occupied Jerusalem, homes are seized and reassigned based entirely on race, and violent settler pogroms are accompanied by Israeli military units. Across the land, Apartheid rules.[6]

From the resignation letter of **Craig Mokhiber**, director of the New York Office of the United Nations High Commissioner for Human Rights (October 28, 2023)

For much of history, *empires* have been the modus operandi of human political experiences. The very idea of a "nation-state," thus coupled, is a by-product of European colonial modernity. The last three empires that ruled over much of the Muslim world—the Mughals, the Safavids to Qajars, and the Ottomans, eventually collapsed and yielded, in their material and moral wherewithal, to the rising power of European empires, the British and the French in particular. The emerging "nation-states" in much of the postcolonial world are the relics and ruins of such fateful encounters. Within the body politic of all nation-states, memories of colliding empires agitate their postcolonial imagination.[7]

Addressing this crucial condition in the context of the Palestinian national liberation movement, scholars contributing to "Palestine Beyond National Frames: Emerging Politics, Cultures, and Claims" (2018) take their inspiration from the towering moral authority of the Polish political activist and a leader of the Warsaw Ghetto Uprising Marek Edelman (circa 1919–2009), who said about his role in those iconic events: "We fought for dignity and freedom, not for territory or a national identity."[8] If we are to take the late Edelman's point as a frame of reference, what is at stake in Palestinian national liberation is something far deeper, something far wider, than just the liberation of Palestine—though that central task must remain definitive to any critical reflection on the past, present, and future of Palestine. Palestinians too have been fighting "for dignity and freedom," and their territorial rootedness in their homeland is the political framing of that struggle.

What exactly is it that goes beyond the frame of "the national"? When we move from the fictive center of "the nation" to the factual trauma of refugee camps where many Palestinians have actually lived after their Nakba, both the operation of states that have occasioned them and the nations trapped within the fictive frontiers of those states are pointedly challenged. Going "beyond" the frame of "the national" always already points back to its very epicenter, where its centrifugal force originates. Right at the very outside of thinking beyond "the national," we need to keep in mind that Palestine is not merely a theoretical proposition. It is a gushing wound. It is a nation without a state, trapped in the colonial vagaries of a European settler-colonial garrison state on the perpetual goose chase of manufacturing a nation for itself.

We know that Palestine has been home to Jews, Christians, and Muslims forever—long before the rise of Zionism as a persistent legacy of European settler colonialism. Palestinians, as a result, are not there to offer political theorists alternative sites of speculative reflections beyond the factual evidence of their history of struggles. They are fighting for their dignity and their homeland, as any other human being would, with audacity and integrity, with courage and imagination, mostly peacefully. In their poetry, film, fiction, and novels, in their scholarship, journalism, and visual and performing arts, in and out of their homeland, subjected to savage occupation and incremental genocide or else living in exile, Palestinians are Palestinians by virtue of the Nakba they have collectively endured. Thinking Palestine beyond its historical borders, therefore, is not an exercise in futility, or worse, weakening our grasp of the resolve of a nation that has suffered too much to dissipate into any postmodern theory. Thinking Palestine beyond the nation must never collapse into disregarding the centrality of a potent national consciousness in the historic making of the Palestinian people and their desire for political liberation.

As such, Palestine has always been integral to any number of other sites of resistance that draw inspiration from Palestinians and see their own struggles in the mirror of their cause. The BDS (Boycott, Divestment, Sanctions) movement is a perfect case in point where the continued struggles of

Palestinians for their national liberation and self-determination thoroughly resonates with the most progressive social movements around the globe, from the Zapatistas in Chiapas, Mexico to Black Lives Matter in the US. "Palestine beyond borders" may be a new theoretical speculation, but it has been a time-honored practice from the very conception of the Palestinian struggle. At the center of the Zionist occupation and continued theft of Palestine, is not merely the fate of millions of Palestinians in and out of their homeland. The historic fate of the Jewish people too is the victim of the selfsame Zionist project. The Zionists are committing astonishing acts of thievery in the name of the Jewish people. The ruling regime in Israel has as much authority representing Jews around the globe as the Islamic State had in representing Muslims, or the US Christian imperialists in representing Christians, or the Hindu fundamentalism of the Bharatiya Janata Party (BJP) Party in representing Hindus. What we have in Israel is the construction of a pure colonial garrison state ruling over Palestinians with brutish violence and unmatched vulgarity, making Palestine a sign and symbol of anticolonial struggles far beyond their own national vicinity.

European colonialism, from which Israeli Zionism is now the most enduring remnant, was not a national project. Predicated on globalized capitalism, it was always a planetary mission, and so has been resistance to it. National liberation movements around the globe, from India to Algeria to Cuba, have always been in structural and practical solidarity with each other. There has never been a progressive political movement anywhere around the globe without active solidarity with Palestinian national liberation. Any national liberation movement by definition must be conscious of the raced, gendered, and classed politics of its own internal dynamics, which in turn makes it structurally connected to similar dynamics in other national liberation movements. One should neither exaggerate nor dismiss the significance of "the national" in the making of a strategic essentialism to resist the perniciously amorphous power of colonialism. Trans- and subnational categories will, therefore, have to be formed within a nation-state, always contingent on a national consciousness as a political frame of reference.

When United Nations authorities responsible for human rights, like Craig Mokhiber and Francesca Albanese, mark the slaughter of Palestinians in horrifying detail, this is the will and the voice of the global community to which Palestine has now become definitive and integral. "Yes, it is genocide," has affirmed Amos Goldberg, a professor of Holocaust history at the Department of Jewish History and Contemporary Jewry at the Hebrew University of Jerusalem: "It is so difficult and painful to admit it, but despite all that, and despite all our efforts to think otherwise, after six months of brutal war we can no longer avoid this conclusion."[9]

The Layered History of the Present Absentee

This is a text-book case of genocide. The European, ethno-nationalist, settler colonial project in Palestine has entered its final phase, toward the expedited destruction of the last remnants of indigenous Palestinian life in Palestine. What's more, the governments of the United States, the United Kingdom, and much of Europe, are wholly complicit in the horrific assault. Not only are these governments refusing to meet their treaty obligations "to ensure respect" for the Geneva Conventions, but they are in fact actively arming the assault, providing economic and intelligence support, and giving political and diplomatic cover for Israel's atrocities.[10]

From the resignation letter of **Craig Mokhiber**, director of the New York Office of the United Nations High Commissioner for Human Rights (October 28, 2023)

Understanding the idea of "Palestine beyond borders" must begin at the epicenter of the critical and creative consciousness of Palestinians to resist the European colonization of their homeland. To reconfigure "the national," therefore, we need not go to the margin and the border of the colonial concoction. We should in fact do precisely the opposite and relocate our critical thinking smack in the middle of the national, but a national that is fully conscious of its always already transnational origin and disposition.[11]

Palestinian artist Emily Jacir spent her childhood in Saudi Arabia before traversing between the US, Europe, and Palestine. That trajectory of Jacir as a migrant artist has been definitive to her work. "But too much of what she does requires wordy explanation before it can be even half understood," a European reviewer of her work has said, before adding, "sometimes, too, her output, partisan and highly political, is closer to activism, even to journalism, than to art."[12] How is one to make a distinction between the artistic and the political in the case of a Palestinian or any other artist for that matter? What should a Palestinian, an Iranian, a Bangladeshi, a Cuban artist do in order to be considered artistic rather than political? Is Picasso's *Guernica* (1937) artistic or political? Is Gillo Pontecorvo's *Battle of Algiers* (1966) a work of art or a work of revolutionary propaganda? What about Goya's *The Third of May 1808* (1814)? How do we make this distinction, or more importantly, why?

This creative and critical encounter between the textured consciousness of a Palestinian artist and the seeming ignorance of a European critic is where the transnational disposition of the Palestinian cause meets the arrested intelligence of a hostile spectatorship. Two aspects of the review of Emily Jacir's work are crucial here: One is the transnational register and aesthetic domain of Jacir's artwork, and the other is the suspicion and vigilance targeted toward her artwork for being Palestinian. A Palestinian artist is at once a rootless cosmopolitan and a suspicious character. She is there to fool you, to pull the wool over the eyes of the innocent and unsuspecting European visitor to her show. There is a pernicious cycle here at work—she is suspicious because she is rootless, and she is rootless because she is suspicious. The moment that a Palestinian, from the heart of her national consciousness, becomes an artist, that suspicion is carried forward to reviews of her artwork.

Like any other artist of her generation, Emily Jacir is the product of a transnational public sphere that enables and disables her at one and the same time, by virtue of not just the predicament but also the privilege of being Palestinian, rooted in a creative effervescence that in her artwork knows and remembers itself. Shirin Neshat was born and raised in Iran, celebrated initially in Europe, and now around the globe. There is not the same level of suspicion against Neshat. In fact, because the evident critique of her own culture dovetails beautifully with the wide-eyed liberalism of many reviewers, Neshat is celebrated for the political undertone of her art. Neshat's presumed politics feeds into the Iranophobia that has defined Western Islamophobia for close to half a century. But not so Emily Jacir's presumed politics, which is wedded, for obvious reasons, to a national liberation movement systematically demonized in the selfsame West.

What is particular about Emily Jacir? Certainly not the fact that her art is "political." Perhaps the issue is that it is political in the wrong way. The subject of Jacir's work, Wael Zuaiter, was a Palestinian writer assassinated by Israel for his supposed affiliation with the Black September group. Even Jacir's reviewer admits that Zuaiter had nothing to do with the killing of Israeli athletes and coaches during the 1972 Summer Olympics. Zuaiter was "politicized" the instant that Israeli assassins murdered him in Rome, apparently firing as many bullets into his body as the number of Israelis killed in Munich, without him having anything to do with what had happened in Munich. According to the reviewer for *The Guardian*:

> It seems odd that the Munich massacre, or any of the other acts committed by Black September, are not detailed in the notes that accompany the work. . . . I couldn't shake off a certain sense of mistrust.[13]

Why is it "odd"? Why should an artist, any artist, Palestinian or otherwise, be burdened with the responsibility of footnoting anything she does with the kind of annotated apology that will satisfy a European spectator? And why does the artist seem suspect if she does not? The European gaze on the textured consciousness of the artist demands to be fully satisfied by the flat diminution of the artist to an absurdist reading of the Palestinian struggle, the majority of it nonviolent and taking the form of peaceful acts of civil disobedience. The irony is that European reviewers politicize the Palestinian artist and then accuse her of being too political. The pernicious absurdity of the act goes to the heart of why the consciousness of the Palestinian artist, rooted in her global resonances, evident in living her nation beyond any and all borders, is constitutionally undecipherable to liberal Western spectatorship—and it must remain that way. That cognitive dissonance is both aesthetically and politically emancipatory.

The reviewer's warning to her readers is critical here: "But keep your eyes and your mind open. This is art as a cause, and it demands not only the visitor's attention, but her hawk-eyed vigilance too."[14] Imagine a full gallery of hawks gathering to watch a Palestinian artist daring to exhibit her work in London. A Palestinian artist is ipso facto suspect, and one must enter her exhibition with eyes wide open, not to see her art, but to see what it is that she is hiding, for she is hiding something. The Palestinian artist, as a result of being precisely a Palestinian artist, becomes a contradiction in terms, an impossibility. The transnational space upon which a Palestinian (artist) is born and her consciousness is formed is definitive to being a Palestinian, at once real in the dispossessed and stateless reality she lives and yet impossible to be visible upon that very transnational space, precisely for being Palestinian.

Must it take a genocide of this magnitude to allow a Palestinian to be seen for what she is and what she does? Can a Palestinian artist be anything but a political artist? And, if so, might we perhaps begin to think of the political not in the way Carl Schmitt saw it, as the site of the constitution of the enemy, but as the birth channel of liberation, a deliverance from the bourgeois morality of siding with the victor and suspecting the victim?

In the Eye of the Palestinian Beholder

In concert with this, western corporate media, increasingly captured and state-adjacent, are in open breach of Article 20 of the ICCPR, continuously dehumanizing Palestinians to facilitate the genocide, and broadcasting propaganda for war and advocacy of national, racial, or religious hatred that constitutes incitement to discrimination, hostility, and violence. US-based social media companies are suppressing the voices of human rights defenders while amplifying pro-Israel propaganda. Israel lobby online-trolls and GONGOS are harassing and smearing human rights defenders, and western universities and employers are collaborating with them to punish those who dare to speak out against the atrocities. In the wake of this genocide, there must be an accounting for these actors as well, just as there was for radio Milles Collines in Rwanda.[15]

From the resignation letter of **Craig Mokhiber**, director of the New York Office of the United Nations High Commissioner for Human Rights (October 28, 2023)

The eyes of a Palestinian artist, as her mind, are always already conscious of a worldly awareness of the nation that translates into her artwork. "The nation" is ipso facto transnational, and the transnational is textured into a layered awareness of the world. The politics of many European critics is blinded to that insight. In that blind spot, the Palestinian artist does not and cannot exist as an artist but only as a prop that is admitted into a European gallery to apologize or Orientalize for what and who she is. The Palestinian artist does not enter "the nation" from that or any other margin; rather, she represents the heart and the center of a national consciousness that has for generations transmuted into a fully aware worldly self-consciousness.

A Palestinian is always suspect in the eyes of her European (or Western) interlocutor. A Palestinian artist is doubly suspicious, for she might do something to that European spectator to make them feel cheated. A Palestinian woman artist is, therefore, trebly anxiety-provoking for a European detective. The result is as much debilitating for the European interlocutor who has repressed their colonial pedigree, as it is, in fact, paradoxically liberating for the Palestinian artist. In that moment of inadmissibility into the domain of approval of the European aesthetic, the Palestinian artist ipso facto reclaims her homeland beyond the recognition or denial of the Western audience. The European is caught between a rock and a hard place, between the atrocities of the Holocaust and the continued calamity of European colonialism now staged in Palestine. The European worries that if she tries to accommodate the memory of the Holocaust, she will perpetuate her colonial history, and, conversely, if she tries to be conscious of the treacherous legacy of colonialism, she might expose the very groundwork of the Jewish Holocaust. But the task ahead is not for us to accommodate the predicament or anxieties of the Western critic beyond their entrapment in this cul-de-sac. The task at hand is mapping out a Palestine without borders into the furthest reaches of our critical imagination. Palestine beyond borders is imagining a world beyond all borders, built on the premises of the most brutalized, the wretched, of this earth.

In that task, we have a way out of the cul-de-sac of the West by turning to the European artist who was never fully European: the Jewish European artist. Was Marc Chagall (1887–1985) also "hiding" something, was he too politicized when attending to the traumas of pogroms and the Holocaust? What is the difference between a European Jewish artist (Chagall) and a Christian Palestinian artist (Jacir)—beyond their respective mediums and manner of their artwork? What do we read when we read a book like *Marc Chagall: The Lost Jewish World* (2006) by Benjamin Harshav? Let us see how Chagall's signature artwork, *The Praying Jew* (1914), is read in specifically formal terms by a leading art critic, Emily Genauer:

> It is immediately apparent that in Vitebsk, working directly from life, the artist was more literal than in Paris where he conjured up Vitebsk from memories. Yet when we examine what at first strikes us as a very "real" portrait, we find evidences of Cubism throughout. Perhaps the most interesting thing about this painting, however, is that Chagall, who generally gives his work emotional impact with brilliant masses of color, here gets his effect by employing large areas of black and white, and by emphasis on the nervous linear patterns, as in the emphasized black straps of the phylactery bound to the arm at right, the black stripes of the prayer shawl, its sawtoothed edge, and the repetition of the traditional curls of hair at each temple, in the curious curl of the dark background above his shoulder at the left. The somber palette, the agitated patterns, and the hunched attitude of the figure, all convey the feelings of an intense and sorrowing man in agonized communion with his God.[16]

CONCLUSION

Writing at the Time of a Genocide

Jews and Palestinians know of broken promises.[1]
James Baldwin, "Open Letter to the Born Again"
(September 29, 1979)

I began writing this book rereading Sven Lindqvist's *"Exterminate All the Brutes": One Man's Odyssey into the Heart of Darkness and the Origins of European Genocide* (1992)—and I am now finishing it while keeping a copy of James Baldwin's *The Fire Next Time* (1963) on my desk. I wonder to myself, is this how people lost their faith when they witnessed the Holocaust? Is this how people trembled when African slaves were brought to these shores in chains? Is this how people closed their eyes in despair when they saw Indigenous people at the mercy of European savageries? Is this how people wept when they saw Congo at the mercy of Belgian barbarism?

I keep reading and rereading Baldwin's passages. I am not Palestinian. But the defiant cry for freedom from injustice and tyranny of all Palestinians has shaped my life. I am not African American. But the beautiful writing of James Baldwin has spoken directly to my soul ever since I set foot on this land in 1976 and read *The Fire Next Time* for the first time. There is a gentleness at the surface of Baldwin's vision and voice, yet his art speaks of hidden horrors. Baldwin's hands burn in fire. I am not surprised at the fact that a genocide of this magnitude and vulgarity could have happened. Far from Gaza, on the edge of this precipice, I have desperately sought the serenity of Baldwin's prose.

"What we are seeing in Gaza is a repeat of Auschwitz," says the Burmese genocide expert and Nobel Peace Prize nominee Maung Zarni. "This is a collective white imperialist man's genocide," he further explains.[2] When Zionists read such comparisons, they become livid. I, on the other hand, committed to the fact of the Jewish Holocaust, find something profoundly liberating in such comparisons, for instead of incarcerating this suffering inside a garrison state, it brings that suffering out into the open, into the fold of humanity, where it rightly belongs. The Jewish Holocaust was a murderous atrocity that Germans and other Europeans perpetrated on defenseless Jews in Europe. The enduring memory of that fact belongs to our entire humanity—and, at this particular moment, to Palestinians. I have argued in this book that what we are witnessing in Gaza and the rest of Palestine is not only an extension of the colonial conquest of the globe. Rather, the genocide we are witnessing is the extension of the normative foundations of a barbarism that has dubbed itself "Western Civilization."

After "the West"

Where do we go from here? The myth and the illusion of "the West" has ended in ignominy, buried forever under the rubble of Gaza. The West was an ideological invention of globalized capitalism. Everything else dubbed "the Rest" was recast by an army of Orientalists in the shadow of that "Western" capitalist modernity. We need to begin with the most brutalized facts on the ground—the Palestinians, the Jews, the Native Americans, all those who have been displaced, all those who are the wretched of the earth. From this premise, a new moral intuition emerges, with its philosophy and political prose embracing us all and reducible to none.

Zionism is a calamitous colonial project abusing the factual memories of generations of Jewish suffering. Judaism and Palestine were both colonized at one and the same time:

Jews robbed of their ancestral faith and Palestinians of their ancestral homeland. Jews have always lived in Palestine and must always have a home in Palestine, next to their Muslim and Christian neighbors. But Jews must also be able to live in peace wherever else they are. American Jews are American, Iranian Jews are Iranian, German Jews are German, and Palestinian Jews are Palestinian. If there are pernicious signs of antisemitism anywhere in the world, and there are, as there is Islamophobia, we need to resist these signs together. The memory of the Holocaust must be liberated from Zionist abuse and wedded to the memories of all other genocidal terror on this earth, particularly to the Palestinian genocide. The specificity of these genocides must be marked but not tribalized. They must be uplifted from a politics of identity and transcended to become the moral cornerstone of a metaphysics of alterity. Palestinians must mark their genocide in Jewish terms, and the Holocaust remembered in decidedly Palestinian terms—both in the active remembering of the Indigenous, African, Latin American, and Asian sufferings endured for millennia.

The Zionist campaign against Palestinians over the last century, which has culminated in the most vicious genocide in Gaza, is the full staging of the political collapse and moral decadence of "Western Civilization." The US and Europe (the West) are not just aiding and abetting Israel during this genocide. Israel has led the West in perpetrating this genocide. This is not to state a mere evident fact. This is a call for rethinking the very metaphysical, the moral and imaginative underpinning of the world after Gaza. The world at large—overcoming the evident divide between the Global South and the Global North, "the West" and "the Rest"—must now begin from the rubbles of Gaza.

In Gaza, what we have witnessed is the complete exposure of the roots of Western Civilization. My contention in this book is that we are not just witness to the demise of Zionism as an ideology of colonial conquest but also to the demise of a Western colonial imagination that originally fathomed and has ever since sustained the settler colony in the form of a garrison state. We could not stop Israel's mass murder of innocent people, but we are capable of exposing the savagery at the roots of that claim to "civilization." To do so, we need to dispense with false premises, flawed nostalgia, entrenched tribalism, and indulgent, self-centering identity politics and look to writers like James Baldwin, who lent his prophetic voice rooted in African American experiences to reading Zionism and Israel as the modus operandi of Western imperialism.

From Said to Magid: Defetishizing "Exile"

The Palestinians have been paying for the British colonial policy of "divide and rule" and for Europe's guilty Christian conscience for more than thirty years.[3]
James Baldwin, "Open Letter to the Born Again"
(September 29, 1979)

During one of my regular visits to Book Culture bookstore on Columbia's campus in New York, I chanced upon a caring, confident, and thoughtful book by Shaul Magid, *The Necessity of Exile: Essays from a Distance* (2023). It grabbed my attention in the midst of the genocide in April 2024. I purchased and began reading the book, and did not put it down until I finished it. Central to the essays collected in this volume is the idea of "exile" specifically in a Jewish context. Written by a professor of Jewish Studies at Dartmouth College, Magid's metaphysical conception of exile is thoroughly biblical and yet cast in decidedly existential and pointedly political terms. Being in exile, Magid seems to suggest, is definitive to Judaism and it ought to remain that way. Soon it becomes evident that the driving force of the thinking behind these essays was Zionism—to be or not to be a Zionist.[4]

Magid arrives at his conclusions from the vantage point of what he terms "counter-Zionism." His essays read like deeply cultivated conversations with many other Zionist, ex-Zionist, post-Zionist, and now counter-Zionist scholars and thinkers, rooted in their Judaic cultures and yet thoroughly conversant with the world they share with the rest of us. I read the book feeling like an interloper standing in the corner of a room where a heated conversation was apace. The interlocutors were entirely oblivious to my presence—though I did not feel particularly unwelcomed. The book reminded me of the glorious poem of the Persian poet Hatef Isfahani (died 1783) in which he depicts a Muslim visiting varieties of religious gatherings, Jewish, Christian, Zoroastrian, and so on—bewildered by what he sees, but ultimately realizing they are all worshiping the selfsame God. So I too sat politely at a margin of the pages and eavesdropped, as it were, on the learned conversation. This is how Magid explains the idea of "counter-Zionism":

> By "counter," I also mean an ideology that resists the ethnocentrism that in my view lies at the very heart of Zionism, which is based on a claim of ownership and thus privilege. Counter-Zionism, free from Zionist ideological claims and proprietary principles, free from the intoxication of power, can provide a vision of nationhood that includes (and does not simply tolerate) ethnic difference. Such a state would not be founded on the notion that "this is our land,

and we will give you a piece of it on our terms"; rather, it would be predicated on the principle that "we live in this land together on equal footing and neither party can claim ownership any more than the other."[5]

Magid has, I thought, a fine liberating idea, which he then proceeds to explain and articulate in more detail. As I was reading these passages, I was, of course, thinking of the unfolding genocide in Gaza. I wondered how these learned scholars would read their own work in the aftermath of the genocide. But I had no way of knowing and proceeded to read. Here is where the political project of "counter-Zionism" became clear:

> What if the concept of shared sovereignty was not perceived as Jews giving away "their" land to Palestinians, but as a recognition of the *equal* rights of Palestinians to the land that is, an acknowledgment that the right of Palestinian self-determination is equal to the right of Jewish self-determination, and that the proprietary nature of the Zionist claim is abolished? ...
>
> In short, what if we shelved Zionism? What if we viewed it, with all its warts and caveats, as an important historical movement in its time, but one that has outlived its purpose? What if we began thinking of

new and different ways to coexist that abandoned the assumed hierarchy of Zionism?[6]

All of these thoughts and "What if's," however, are geared toward the idea of exile. Here is how he puts it: "In many ways, Zionism as a political and religious ideology is founded on this negation of exile: For Zionism to make sense, Jewish exile needs to be a 'problem' for which Zionism is the solution."[7] From which premise Magid reflects on Rav Shagar's views of exile as a "positive and constructive notion" that acts "as a humbling force that enabled Jews to develop a deeply empathetic and ethical posture toward the world and toward themselves."[8] In his writing, I sensed a liberating conception of "exile," whereby Jews would stand against, or as Magid prefers to say, "counter" to Zionism.

What I found utterly mesmerizing about this book and Magid's preoccupation with the issue of "exile" in a "counter-Zionist" argument was how close his thinking is to Edward Said's almost identical conception of exile, though in his case from a decidedly "secular" point of view. Why would pointedly Jewish thinking about exile be so similar to a professedly secular conception of it? Of course, the answer is Palestine. Both Magid and, before him, Said were preoccupied with Palestine and the land that both Palestinians and Jews (not Zionists) have a claim to. The Christian Palestinian scholar (Said) and the Jewish scholar (Magid) are both talking about

Palestine, though one in a professedly Jewish and the other in a manifestly secular, yet most emphatically evident, Christian sense. Though born and raised a Christian, Said made a theoretical point of confessing to be secular.[9] And yet, when it came to the exilic condition, his thinking was almost identical with these post- or counter-Zionist thinkers. Here is how Said puts his conception of "exile":

> While it is an *actual* condition, exile is also for my purposes a *metaphorical* condition. By that I mean that my diagnosis of the intellectual in exile derives from the social and political history of dislocation and migration with which I began this lecture, but is not limited to it. Even intellectuals who are lifelong members of a society can, in a manner of speaking, be divided into insiders and outsiders: those on the one hand who belong fully to the society as it is, who flourish in it without an overwhelming sense of dissonance or dissent, those who can be called yea-sayers; and on the other hand, the nay-sayers, the individuals at odds with their society and therefore outsiders and exiles so far as privileges, power, and honors are concerned.[10]

This idea of Said's, I have always thought, was a self-projection. As a Palestinian, this is how he saw himself. "The pattern that sets the course for the intellectual as outsider," Said further explains, "is best exemplified by the condition of exile, the state of never being fully adjusted, always feeling outside the chatty, familiar world inhabited by natives, so to speak, tending to avoid and even dislike the trappings of accommodation and national well-being."[11] This, to be sure, he did not mean in an abstract sense, but in a very real and tangible way, which he still considered "metaphysical": "Exile for the intellectual in this metaphysical sense is restlessness, movement, constantly being unsettled, and unsettling others. You cannot go back to some earlier and perhaps more stable condition of being at home; and, alas, you can never fully arrive, be at one with your new home or situation."[12] Magid draws his conception of exile from the depth of his Jewish doctrinal history, and Said from the lived experiences of a Palestinian who, too, cannot ever go back home to his parental (occupied) homeland. But, still, they are both celebrating the condition of exile, which they believe to be more in line with who and what they are: a stateless Palestinian and an existentially exilic Jew.

Though existential and rooted, both these accounts of "exile" seem to be creating a decidedly fetishized conception of it, something epiphenomenal. A Palestinian critical thinker and a Jewish critical thinker, who on the surface might be perceived as each other's nemesis, share an identical sense of homelessness.[13] Their ideas of exile are rooted in the question of Palestine, yet perhaps precisely because of that, the idea is existentially, conceptually, and metaphysically reified. Since my first reading of Said on exile in his seminal book on *Representations of the Intellectual* (1994), I have always disagreed with his nostalgic and existential uprootedness.[14] There is no home left anywhere to be exiled from—I have always thought. The earth is shattering and dwindling. If I were to go back to Iran, I'll feel "in exile," not in New York, where I have meaning and purpose and a confident voice in my life. Home is where we hang our hat and say no to power. I think we are liberated from the idea of exile, for we are at home on a very fragile planet.[15]

To be sure, I have deep sympathy for Magid's articulation of the idea of "counter-Zionism." I have a similar trajectory in my own work, overcoming the Islamist project of the last two hundred years in what is now considered a "post-Islamist" state of thinking and being. But the idea of "exile," in the writing of both Said and Magid, I find inimical or at least counterproductive to this project. In my *Brown Skin, White Masks* (2011), I took Said's conception of the exilic intellectual to task, for I did not think it useful and, in fact, thought it decidedly debilitating in our current conception of the world. Comprador intellectuals were also the product of this sense of exilic intellectuals; certainly not all exilic intellectuals were like Said or Magid. The notorious Lebanese reactionary Fouad Ajami and many Islamophobic Zionists who believe Israel is their home but live in the US are also "in exile." The late Said and Magid must abandon the idea of exile and just be at home where they are.

I recall thinking when writing *Brown Skin, White Masks* that some people are American because they were born to American parents in this country, while others become American because American children are born to them. I was born and I remain Iranian, though my address changed from my hometown in southern Iran, to my undergraduate years in Tehran, to where I work on Columbia's campus now. I have desired a different kind of organicity of the intellectual, beyond political boundaries. I recall thinking that I cannot allow a Zionist like Daniel Pipes or David Horowitz, with their roots in Poland or Russia, to think themselves "American," with a sense of ownership and entitlement to this country, while I remain marginal to it. Instead of a marginal intellectual, I suggested the idea of "amphibian intellectuals," thinking in and in between two or more languages and cultures.

Be that as it may, what astonishes me about Magid's discussion of Zionism or even "counter-Zionism" is how he and all his interlocutors are so oblivious to the misery Zionism has inflicted on Palestinians or the hostile environment in which the British planted their Israel. It is all so abstract and biblical: Exile or no exile, sharing or not sharing the land. It is so deeply biblical that it turns out to be, in fact, entirely historical! As I write in early August 2024, Israel is fighting on several fronts. Even if we were to forget about Palestinians, what sort of security does that offer Jews, or what sort of future? Israel is a dysfunctional killing machine—it could not possibly be anyone's homeland unless there is a radical shift in perspective, which is not biblical but begins with the ruins of Gaza and builds up to a semblance of humanity.

I finish this line of thinking on Magid and Said remembering a particularly powerful scene in Richard Attenborough's movie *Gandhi* (1982), where Mahatma Gandhi is on hunger strike, protesting communal violence between Muslims and Hindus. At one point, an angry Hindu man comes to plead with him to eat—and to convince him, this dialogue ensues:

> **Nahari:** I'm going to Hell! I killed a child! I smashed his head against a wall.
>
> **Gandhi:** Why?
>
> **Nahari:** Because they killed my son! The Muslims killed my son!
>
> **Gandhi:** I know a way out of Hell. Find a child, a child whose mother and father have been killed and raise him as your own.

The man seems to be convinced and is about to leave. Gandhi is not done yet:

Gandhi: Only be sure that he is a Muslim and that you raise him as one.

In that moment, the entirety of humanity was a Muslim child, a Jewish child, a Hindu child, all summoned up today in a Palestinian child killed by Israeli soldiers. We are past the delusions of exile.

Before and After the Genocide

I am in the strenuous and far from dull position of having news to deliver to the Western world—for example: black is not a synonym for slave. Do not, I counsel you, attempt to defend yourselves against this stunning, unwieldy and undesired message. You will hear it again: indeed, this is the only message the Western world is likely to be hearing from here on out.[16]
James Baldwin, "Open Letter to the Born Again" (September 29, 1979)

It is impossible to think of the world after the genocide in Gaza as we did before the genocide in Gaza. It is a different world—not just because of the enormity and brazenness of how Israel has treated Palestinians. It is a different world because Zionism has exposed, for the whole world to see, what European colonialism has done to the world for over five hundred years. The succession of massacres in Gaza and the Palestinian genocide form a threshold similar to the moral and philosophical consequences of the Jewish Holocaust in European intellectual history. Just as after the Jewish Holocaust, the entire project of European Enlightenment modernity was put under scrutiny and systematically dismantled; in the aftermath of the Palestinian genocide, the philosophical project of a post-Western world commences in earnest. Just as in the aftermath of Auschwitz, when the Frankfurt School, Critical Theory, and varied shades of postmodernism and poststructuralism emerged, Gaza must become the ground zero of a world liberated from the illusion of the West and all its fabricated binaries. Through its genocidal Zionism, the West has finally self-imploded and the entire edifice of Western Philosophy exposed for the brutish tribalism it had managed violently to conceal and universalize. Gaza has deuniversalized the West and exposed its tribal and ethnic roots. From now on, we neither celebrate nor denounce, neither center nor decenter, the West. We need not even "provincialize" it. The West has had its historical course and died in Gaza. Palestine is now the epicenter of our emerging modes of knowledge production, of knowing who and what the rest of our humanity might be.

From under the ruins of Gaza do not emerge categories and concepts, let alone theories and philosophies. From under the ruins of Gaza emerges nothing but dead bodies, broken bones, pieces of flesh. The weight of that rubble will forever be on the record of Western civilization and the garrison state it created and called Israel. Fragmented bones and torn flesh, bodies in mass graves become the living allegories of the moral categories we were denied. There and then, we start as nothing but Palestinians. We are not Arabs, Muslims, Orientals, or any other names we were called. We are allegorical allusions to what we were never allowed to be: total human beings. We dwell on that intransigent impossibility of becoming fully human or fully animal. We need to take the words of our mass murderers quite literally—and not metaphorically.

Where is the site of salvation? How do we begin to heal at the sight of the enormity of the pain Palestinians have endured? Gaza is now the site of our moral imperatives, the political shape of the future to come. From the ruins of Gaza, we must begin building a new imagination in which the West has absolutely no moral authority. "The West" is the code of a global criminality—not just because it has subjected the world to unspeakable savagery as Israel now does in Palestine, but because it calls itself a "civilization."

It is not a civilization. It is barbarism manifest: from its philosophy to its politics, to its humanism. Israel, the self-proclaimed "Jewish state," is on trial for genocide. Its leaders are charged with crimes against humanity. The Zionist regime in charge has always been a Jewish supremacist apartheid system, actively engaged in ethnic cleansing, mass detentions, targeted extra-juridical assassinations, gender-based violence, and torture.

The self-confessed crisis of "Western philosophy" is the solid evidence of this moral depravity in epistemic terms. Today, the crisis of European philosophy *is* European philosophy. Consider the edited volume *After Philosophy: End or Transformation?* (1987) and try to read it in the aftermath of the Palestinian genocide. Here you see how eminent and professional European and American ("Western") philosophers have made a long and illustrious career out of not knowing what philosophy is. Some fourteen philosophers have gathered here, all Europeans and Americans, to define philosophy at the moment of its irretrievable crisis. It is not accidental that they are all Europeans and Americans. The rest of us have no "philosophy"—and rightly so, for this calamity in detailed ontological and epistemological terms is entirely European and Western. From Richard Rorty and Jean-François Lyotard to Michel Foucault, Jacques Derrida, Hans-Georg Gadamer, Paul Ricoeur, Alasdair MacIntyre, Hans Blumenberg, and Charles Taylor, we read one towering contemporary European and American philosopher after another, chasing after each other in circles, and not a single one of them has anything to say outside that spiral of their own self-indulgent preoccupations. Not a single word they have said in this seminal volume has any relevance to or about the calamity the world has witnessed for a century in Palestine, at the mercy of their "Western civilization."

We, the rest of the world, the world that has been "rested" by these philosophers, have a place of origin furthest removed from them. For now, and for any future to unfold, Gaza must become the metaphor that stands for the entirety of Palestine and for the entirety of what is left of our humanity. Two books immediately suggest themselves as the model of critical thinking for a radically different mode of knowledge production to come: Helga Tawil-Souri and Dina Matar's edited volume *Gaza as Metaphor* (2016) and Nadia Yaqub's edited volume *Gaza on Screen* (2023). Precisely in their kaleidoscopic vision, they represent the best we can imagine. These books represent the luminous fragments of thinking pointedly and allegorically about Gaza as the simulacrum of Palestine and as the metaphor of our world at large.

God in Gaza

Write it down!
I am an Arab![17]

Mahmoud Darwish, "*Bitaqah Huwiyyah /*
Identity Card" (1964)

There is no thinking beyond "Western philosophy" without thinking beyond the entrapment of Arabs and Muslims in a closed-circuited ritualism bereft of any meaning in the aftermath of the genocide. In the midst of relentless news from Palestine, day after day and month after month, the realization that Hajj had just commenced in June 2024 came to me as an afterthought, with a sense of wonder. Performing the pilgrimage of Hajj is a precious article of faith that not all Muslims have the privilege of completing. My late parents, both devout Muslims each in their own unique way, left this world unable to perform that joyous duty. Regularly traveling from our hometown Ahvaz to Qom and Mashhad as pilgrims to the mausoleums of Shi'i saints and imams was the closest they ever came to the idea, for they could scarce afford going to Najaf and Karbala in Iraq, let alone Mecca and Medina in Saudi Arabia.

We Muslims believe God is everywhere, that He is closer to us than our jugular vein or *habl al-warid*, as we read in the Qur'an. But today, like all other human beings, our veins and our breathing pulsates in Palestine. If God were to be anywhere in particular, would He not be in the vicinity of an emaciated body of a child intentionally starved to death in Gaza?

All I could think of as I read the news of Muslim pilgrims in Arabia was Rumi's (1207–1273) poem that starts with these iconic lines:

> *Ey Qom-e beh Haj rafteh koja'id koja'id ...*
> O people who have gone to Hajj, where are you; where are you?
> The Beloved is right here, come hither, come hither![18]

The ghazal continues to remind Muslims that the Beloved (a precious allusion to God) they seek is right here and is, in fact, their next-door neighbor. Why do they bother to get lost in the desert trying to reach Him? If Muslims were to realize the formless form of the Divine, Rumi says, they would know that they are themselves the Master, the House, and the House of Kaaba they seek. Referring to Kaaba as the House of God, Rumi writes:

> Time and again you have traveled highways to get to that House—
> Just once ascend your own house and come to the roof!
> Yes that House is precious you know all its signs—
> But just once show a sign of the Master of that House!

> You would not be content with just a bouquet of flower
> if you were to see that garden,
> One precious stone would not matter if you were from
> the Sea of His Divinity!

Rumi writes of eternal love—but how do we read him today in the deepest despair of hate that pours death and destruction over Muslims and Christians alike in Palestine? Where is God—the Muslim God, the Christian God, the Jewish God—these days? Rumi concludes his poem painfully—and so must I:

> Be that as it may, may your troubles be amply rewarded
> Though alas you are the veil on your own treasures!

There is a post-Islamist liberation theology that will flourish alongside a post-Zionist Jewish liberation theology. In anticipation of that eventuality, Palestine remains as the abiding metaphor, a guiding light, showing us the way.

ACKNOWLEDGMENTS

The writing of this book has been a particularly tasking endeavor—writing on a genocide as the genocide is happening. Without the steady care and the wise counsel of my editor Brekhna Aftab, this book would not have the point of departure and delivery that it now does. I sent her a crescendo of thoughts and a steady stream of critical thinking based on incontrovertible facts and documented atrocities, from which she carefully and patiently carved and crafted this book and let the precise purpose of my intentions come through. She is a blessing to have as an editor. To the entire editorial collective of Haymarket Books goes my enduring gratitude.

My dear editors at *Middle East Eye*, Omayma Abdel-Latif, Leena Al-Arian, and Megan O'Toole are instrumental in my regular musings on our current world affairs. I am grateful to them for allowing my voice to be part of the global chorus for truth and justice.

Dozens of brave, dedicated, and principled Palestinian journalists have been murdered in Gaza and elsewhere in Palestine in order for the world to glimpse the terror an entire nation has been suffering at the hands of Israel, and the US- and European-made weapons of mass destruction put at Israel's disposal. Without these journalists risking their lives, the world would have been blind to the facts of the genocide. No scholar or critical thinker anywhere in the world can write a serious sentence about Palestine without the sacrifices of courageous journalists like Shireen Abu Akleh (1971–2022), who was cold-bloodedly murdered by the Israeli occupation forces while reporting on one of their countless crimes against humanity.

To countless Palestinian friends and colleagues throughout their homeland, from Gaza to the West Bank to inside the 1948 borders or exiled around the world, goes my heartfelt gratitude for giving me the privilege to witness their dignity and inspiring courage. To Nizar Hasan in Nazareth, Elia Suleiman, Najwa Najjar, Hany Abu-Assad, and Kamal Aljafari in and out of Palestine, Mai Masri in Lebanon, Ismail Nashef in Doha, and countless other dearest friends and colleagues goes my particular gratitude for keeping me in the confidence of their trust.

To my Lebanese, Syrian, Egyptian, and Moroccan friends in Beirut, Damascus, Cairo, and Rabat, I owe my most cherished memories of many visits basking in their kind and generous hospitalities: Fawwaz Traboulsi, the late Samah Idriss, the late Elias Khoury, George Saliba, Ahmad Dallal, Elizabeth Kassab, and Rasha Salti.

In Doha, my gratitude to Yasir Suleiman-Malley, Abdelwahab El-Affendi, Safwan Masri, Ayman El-Desouky, Eid Mohammad, Atef Botros al-Attar, Ibrahim Fraihat, Adham Saouli, Tariq Dana, Mohamad Hamas Elmasry, and countless others.

For a lifetime of friendship and a model of principled resistance and tireless institution building, special thanks to Azmi Bishara, to our precious memories together from New York to Doha; Marwan Bishara, for his defiant soul and matchless scholarship; to my dear friend Ilan Pappé, my everlasting gratitude.

In Berlin, my sister Mahfarid Mansourian; in Paris, my old friend Anissa Bouziane; in Mexico City, my solid comrades Moisés Garduño García and Alejandra Gómez Colorado; in Victoria, Canada, Peyman Vahabzadeh; in Seoul, Siavash Saffari; in Leiden, Marina Calculli; in Amsterdam, Peyman Jafari and Miranda Lakerveld; in London, Daryoush Mohammad Poor; in New York, Ramin Bahrani and Karim Malak; in New Jersey, Samah Selim and Alamin Mazrui; on Instagram, Najla Said . . . impossible to even list the precious names of friends and colleagues who in person or in spirit have held my hand steady as I wrote this testimonial to the ungodly suffering and yet defiant soul of Palestinians.

From the river to the sea . . .

NOTES

Preface: "Exterminate All the Brutes," Again!
1. Joseph Conrad, *Heart of Darkness and The Congo Diary*, ed. Robert Hampson and Owen Knowles (London: Penguin Classics, 2007), 92.
2. "Israeli Lawmaker's 'Kill All Palestinians' Remarks Resurface," *Daily Sabah*, May 16, 2021, https://www.dailysabah.com/world/mid-east/israeli-lawmakers-kill-all-palestinians-remarks-resurface.
3. Sven Lindqvist, *"Exterminate All the Brutes": One Man's Odyssey into the Heart of Darkness and the Origins of European Genocide*, trans. Joan Tate (New York: The New Press, 1992), ix.
4. Aimé Césaire, *Discourse on Colonialism*, trans. Joan Pinkham (New York: Monthly Review, 1950), 36.
5. Sarah Fortinsky, "Israel's President Defends Ongoing War: 'If It Weren't for Us, Europe Would Be Next,'" *The Hill*, December 5, 2023, https://thehill.com/policy/international/4343274-israels-president-defends-ongoing-war-if-it-werent-for-us-europe-would-be-next/.
6. This particular phase of Israeli genocide of Palestinians is in the context of a longer history best documented by the

eminent historian Ilan Pappé, *The Ethnic Cleansing of Palestine* (London: Oneworld, 2007).
7. Hamid Dabashi, "Thanks to Gaza, European Philosophy Has Been Exposed as Ethically Bankrupt," *Middle East Eye*, January 18, 2024, https://www.middleeasteye.net/opinion/war-gaza-european-philosophy-ethically-bankrupt-exposed; Nicole Deitelhoff, Rainer Forst, Klaus Günther, and Jürgen Habermas, "Principles of Solidarity. A Statement," November 13, 2023, Normative Orders, https://www.normativeorders.net/2023/grundsatze-der-solidaritat/.
8. Hamid Dabashi, "Gaza: Poetry After Auschwitz," Al Jazeera, August 8, 2014, https://www.aljazeera.com/opinions/2014/8/8/gaza-poetry-after-auschwitz.
9. Hamid Dabashi, *Can Non-Europeans Think?* (London: Zed Books, 2015).
10. "Defense Minister Announces 'Complete Siege' of Gaza: No Power, Food or Fuel," *The Times of Israel*, https://www.timesofisrael.com/liveblog_entry/defense-minister-announces-complete-siege-of-gaza-no-power-food-or-fuel/.
11. Giorgio Agamben, *Remnants of Auschwitz: The Witness and the Archive* (New York: Zone Books, 1999), 17.
12. *Middle East Eye* staff, "Naji al-Ali Remembered: A Palestinian Cartoonist Gunned Down in London," *Middle East Eye*, August 30, 2022, https://www.middleeasteye.net/discover/palestine-naji-ali-handala-creator-remembered.
13. For a solid history of Palestinian dispossession, see Rashid Khalidi, *The Hundred Years' War on Palestine* (New York: Metropolitan Books, 2021). For a cogent critic of the Israeli atrocities over the decades, see Azmi Bishara, *Palestine: Matters of Truth and Justice* (London: Hurst, 2022).
14. Deitelhoff et al., "Principles of Solidarity."
15. Patrick Wolfe, "Settler Colonialism and the Elimination of

the Native," *Journal of Genocide Research* 8, no. 4 (December 2006): 387–409, https://kooriweb.org/foley/resources/pdfs/89.pdf.
16. Samar L. Kasim, "Israel's Former Ambassador to UN Calls Palestinians 'Inhuman Animals,'" Andalou Agency, October 27, 2023, https://www.aa.com.tr/en/middle-east/israel-s-former-ambassador-to-un-calls-palestinians-inhuman-animals/3034022#:~:text=Former%20Israeli%20ambassador%20to%20the,a%20tightened%20blockade%20on%20Gaza.
17. For a classic text on the enduring moral question of Palestine, see Edward Said, *The Question of Palestine* (New York: Penguin Random House, 1992). For a sequel to the same issues, see Joseph Massad, *The Persistence of the Palestinian Question* (London: Routledge, 2006).
18. For a solid exposition of the Israeli settler colony's military origin, see Haim Bresheeth-Zabner, *An Army Like No Other: How the Israel Defense Force Made a Nation* (London and New York: Verso, 2020).
19. Immanuel Kant, *Groundwork of the Metaphysics of Morals*, trans. and ed. Mary Gregor (Cambridge, UK: Cambridge University Press, 1997), 31.
20. Hamid Dabashi, *The End of Two Illusions: Islam After the West* (Oakland: University of California Press, 2022).
21. Immanuel Kant, *Observations on the Feeling of the Beautiful and Sublime*, trans. John T. Goldthwait (Oakland: University of California Press, 1961/2003), 111.
22. Ilan Ben Zio, Associated Press, "Israeli Crowds Chant Racist Slogans, Taunt Palestinians During Jerusalem Day March," PBS News, May 18, 2023, https://www.pbs.org/newshour/world/israeli-crowds-chant-racist-slogans-taunt-palestinians-during-jerusalem-day-march.

23. Primo Levi, *If This Is a Man / Survival in Auschwitz* (New York: Touchstone, 1958/1993), 9.
24. United Nations, Office for the Coordination of Humanitarian Affairs – Occupied Palestinian Territory, "Remarks to the Security Council by Sigrid Kaag, Senior Humanitarian and Reconstruction Coordinator for Gaza," April 24, 2024, https://www.ochaopt.org/content/remarks-security-council-sigrid-kaag-senior-humanitarian-and-reconstruction-coordinator-gaza.
25. Ghassan Kanafani, "Letter from Gaza" (1956), available online online at https://www.marxists.org/archive/kanafani/1956/letterfromgaza.htm. For a discussion of this "Letter," see Hisham Matter, "Letter from Gaza," Granta, May 11, 2009, https://granta.com/letter-from-gaza/.

Chapter 1: Palestine Is the World; the World Is Palestine

1. For a detailed discussion, see Mohammed El-Kurd, "Are We Indeed All Palestinians?" *Mondoweis*, March 13, 2024, https://mondoweiss.net/2024/03/are-we-indeed-all-palestinians/.
2. For a more detailed discussion, see Hamid Dabashi, "Israel-Palestine War: Reclaiming the Slogan 'From the River to the Sea,'" *Middle East Eye*, December 2, 2023, https://www.middleeasteye.net/opinion/israel-palestine-war-reclaiming-slogan-river-sea.
3. Esmat Elhalaby, "The World of Edward Said," *Boston Review*, May 13, 2021, https://bostonreview.net/philosophy-religion/esmat-elhalaby-world-edward-said.
4. Elhalaby, "World of Edward Said."
5. For the most recent study of Israel as a settler colony, see Jeff Halper, *Decolonizing Israel, Liberating Palestine: Zionism,*

Settler Colonialism, and the Case for One Democratic State (London: Pluto Press, 2021).
6. For a cogent critique of the idea of "world literature," see Emily Apter, *Against World Literature: On the Politics of Untranslatability* (New York: Verso, 2014). For a more radical critique of the idea of "world literature" because of its imperial and colonial pedigree, see Hamid Dabashi, *The Shahnameh: The Persian Epic as World Literature* (New York: Columbia University Press, 2019).
7. For a cogent critic of the field from within the field, see Gayatri Chakravorty Spivak, *Death of a Discipline* (New York: Columbia University Press, 2005).
8. David Damrosch, *What Is World Literature?* (Princeton, NJ: Princeton University Press, 2003), 282.
9. For a cogent critique of this interface, see Baidik Bhattacharya, *Postcolonial Writing in the Era of World Literature: Texts, Territories, Globalizations* (London: Routledge, 2019).
10. In *Continental Philosophy and the Palestinian Question: Beyond the Jew and the Greek* (London: Bloomsbury Academic, 2017), Zahi Zalloua has started asking these sorts of questions.
11. For a key text on this transformative power of Palestine as a site of critical knowledge production, see Azmi Bishara's magisterial study, *Palestine: Matters of Truth and Justice* (London: Hurst, 2022).
12. Maurizio Passerin D'Entreves and Seyla Benhabib, eds., *Habermas and the Unfinished Project of Modernity: Critical Essays on the Philosophical Discourse of Modernity* (Cambridge, MA: MIT Press, 1997).
13. In *Europe and Its Shadows: Coloniality After Empire* (London: Pluto Press, 2019), I have detailed the dialectical disposition

of the "Europe" metaphor and its moral and imaginative others colonially construed.
14. For the most recent collection of essays addressing this global solidarity from the vantage point of indigeneity, see Suzannah Henty and Gary Foley, "Indigenous Solidarity: Testimonies and Narratives," *28 Magazine*, August 2021, https://www.28mag.ps/wp-content/uploads/2021/08/Palestinians-and-Indigenous-Peoples-Testimonies-and-Narratives-on-Solidarity-28-Magazine-11092021.pdf.
15. I proposed the idea of "delayed defiance" when I wrote *The Arab Spring: The End of Postcolonialism* (London: Zed Books, 2012), on the revolutionary aspirations of the Arab Spring.
16. For a sample of his literary output, see Ghassan Kanafani, *Men in the Sun and Other Palestinian Stories,* trans. Hilary Kilpatrick (Boulder, CO: Lynne Rienner, 1999).
17. To learn more about "My Dear Lamis / The Little Lantern," the video Mario Rizzi made about Anni Kanafani, see "Mario Rizzi," Dar El-Nimer, https://www.darelnimer.org/past-events/my-dear-lamis-by-mario-rizzi. On multiple occasions, including in this case, Rizzi has invited me to write on his work for major exhibitions where his artwork is first exhibited.
18. In my edited volume on Palestinian cinema, *Dreams of a Nation: On Palestinian Cinema* (New York: Verso, 2006), I call this a "mimetic crisis" at the heart of Palestinian cinema.
19. The play was also turned into a musical in 2004. For more details, see "Al-Fawanees": The First Musical in Palestine," available online at: http://miftah.org/Display.cfm?DocId=4418&CategoryId=32.
20. Mahmoud Darwish, "No More and No Less," in *The Butterfly's Burden*, trans. Fady Joudah (Port Townsend, WA: Copper Canyon Press, 2007), https://www.poetryfoundation.org/poems/52548/no-more-and-no-less.

Chapter 2: Israel Is "the West"; "the West" Is Israel

1. United Nations, Office of the High Commissioner for Human Rights, "UN Experts Declare Famine Has Spread Throughout Gaza Strip," press release, July 9, 2024, https://www.ohchr.org/en/press-releases/2024/07/un-experts-declare-famine-has-spread-throughout-gaza-strip.
2. Ilan Pappé, *The Biggest Prison on Earth: A History of the Occupied Territories* (London: Oneworld, 2017), 1.
3. Pappé, *Biggest Prison on Earth*, 1.
4. Ilan Pappé, *The Ethnic Cleansing of Palestine* (London: Oneworld, 2007), 10.
5. Application of the Convention on the Prevention and Punishment of the Crime of Genocide in the Gaza Strip (*South Africa v. Israel*), December 29, 2023. Available on the official website of the International Court of Justice at: https://www.icj-cij.org/case/192/written-proceedings.
6. Maxime Rodinson, *Israel: A Colonial Settler-State?* (New York: Monad Press, 1973).
7. Rodinson, *Israel: A Colonial Settler-State?*, 91.
8. Arghiri Emmanuel, "White-Settler Colonialism and the Myth of Investment Imperialism," *New Left Review* 1, no. 73 (May–June 1972): 35–57.
9. Lorenzo Veracini, "The Other Shift: Settler Colonialism, Israel, and the Occupation," *Journal of Palestine Studies* 42, no. 2 (2013): 26–42.
10. Tariq Dana and Ali Jarbawi, "A Century of Settler Colonialism in Palestine: Zionism's Entangled Project," *The Brown Journal of World Affairs* 24, no. 1 (Fall/Winter 2017): 197–220.
11. Dana and Jarbawi, "Century of Settler Colonialism."
12. Dana and Jarbawi, "Century of Settler Colonialism."
13. Patrick Wolfe, "Settler Colonialism and the Elimination of the Native," *Journal of Genocide Research* 8, no. 4 (2006): 387–409.

14. David Lloyd and Patrick Wolfe, "Settler colonial logics and the neoliberal regime,". *Settler Colonial Studies* 6, no. 2 (2015): 109–18, https://doi.org/10.1080/220147 3X.2015.1035361.
15. Lloyd and Wolfe, "Settler Colonial Logics."
16. Ilan Pappé, "Zionism as Colonialism: A Comparative View of Diluted Colonialism in Asia and Africa," *South Atlantic Quarterly* 107, no. 4 (Fall 2008): 612.
17. Pappé, "Zionism as Colonialism," 612.
18. Pappé, "Zionism as Colonialism," 612–13
19. Pappé, "Zionism as Colonialism," 613
20. Lindqvist, *"Exterminate All the Brutes,"* 8.
21. United Nations, "Commission of Inquiry on the Occupied Palestinian Territory Concludes that Israeli Authorities and Hamas Are Both Responsible for War Crimes—UN Human Rights Council," June 19, 2024, https://www.un.org/unispal/document/commission-of-inquiry-pr-hrc-19jun24/.
22. Francesca Albanese, *Anatomy of a Genocide*, Report of the Special Rapporteur on the Situation of Human Rights in the Palestinian Territory Occupied Since 1967, the United Nations, March 24, 2024, https://www.un.org/unispal/document/anatomy-of-a-genocide-report-of-the-special-rapporteur-on-the-situation-of-human-rights-in-the-palestinian-territory-occupied-since-1967-to-human-rights-council-advance-unedited-version-a-hrc-55/.
23. Gabriel Rockhill, "The CIA and the Frankfurt School's Anti-Communism," *Monthly Review*, July 6, 2022, https://mronline.org/2022/07/06/the-cia-the-frankfurt-schools-anti-communism/.
24. Stuart Jeffries, *Grand Hotel Abyss* (New York: Verso, 2016): 297.
25. Rockhill, "CIA and the Frankfurt's School Anti-Communism."
26. Rockhill, "CIA and the Frankfurt's School Anti-Communism."

27. Theodor Adorno and Max Horkheimer, *Towards a New Manifesto*, trans. Rodney Livingstone (New York: Verso, 2011), 40–41.
28. Rockhill, "CIA and the Frankfurt's School Anti-Communism."
29. Antonio Y. Vázquez-Arroyo, "Critical Theory, Colonialism, and the Historicity of Thought," *Constellations* 25, no. 1 (2018): 54–70.
30. Vázquez-Arroyo, "Critical Theory, Colonialism," 55.
31. Amy Allen, *The End of Progress: Decolonizing the Normative Foundations of Critical Theory* (New York: Columbia University Press, 2016), 2–3.
32. Rev. Dr. Munther Isaac, "Christ in the Rubble: A Liturgy of Lament," Evangelical Lutheran Christmas Church Bethlehem, December 23, 2023, https://redletterchristians.org/2023/12/23/christ-in-the-rubble-a-liturgy-of-lament/. I first developed this idea of "Palestinian liberation theology" in this short essay (which I now revise and expand here): "War on Gaza Pits Palestinian Liberation Theology Against Evangelical Zionism," *Middle East Eye*, February 5, 2024, https://www.middleeasteye.net/opinion/war-gaza-palestinian-liberation-theology-zionism-evangelical.
33. See Enrique Dussel, *Philosophy of Liberation*, trans. Aquilina Martinez and Christine Morkovsky (New York: Orbis Books, 1980).
34. Isaac, "Christ in the Rubble."
35. For more on this iconography, see Hamid Dabashi, "The Iconography of Palestinian Martyrdom," *Middle East Eye*, June 2, 2022, https://www.middleeasteye.net/opinion/palestinian-iconography-martyrdom.
36. See Robert N. Bellah, "Civil Religion in America," in "Religion in America," special issue, *Dædalus* 96, no. 1 (Winter 1967): 1–21.

37. Bartolomé de las Casas, *A Short Account of the Destruction of the Indies* (London: Penguin Books, 1999).
38. Hamid Dabashi, *The Last Muslim Intellectual: The Life and Legacy of Jalal Al-e Ahmad* (Edinburgh: Edinburgh University Press, 2021).
39. Peter Beinart, "The Great Rupture in American Jewish Life," *New York Times*, March 22, 2024, https://www.nytimes.com/2024/03/22/opinion/israel-american-jews-zionism.html?smid=nytcore-ios-share&referringSource=articleShare&sgrp=c-cb.
40. Solid works of scholarship on Jewish Holocaust abound, but still, Raul Hilberg's three-volume opus *The Destruction of the European Jews* (New Haven: Yale University Press, 2003) remains exemplary in its solid documentations.
41. Beinart, "Great Rupture."
42. To be clear, Peter Beinart is not the only ex-Zionist boldly articulating such positions. This seems to be an endemic phenomenon among the most critical Jewish thinkers today, as it has, of course, always been since Hannah Arendt. Equally important but still perplexing is Joshua Leifer in his newly published *Tablets Shattered: The End of an American Jewish Century and the Future of a Jewish Life* (New York: Penguin Random House, 2024). Here, we read how young American Zionists had built a sandcastle for themselves where what they called "Americanism, Zionism, and liberalism" lived happily ever after. What is astonishing about these heartfelt memoires is the willful neglect, a purposeful blindness to the suffering of Palestinians, that this delusional Zionism had opted to ignore. Palestinians did not exist, their suffering did not matter, the dispossession of their homeland did not count for this entire generation of self-deluding Zionists. For an excerpt from Leifer's book, see "In my youth, Judaism and Zionism felt synonymous. Now

the American Jewish consensus has collapsed," *The Guardian*, August 15, 2024, https://www.theguardian.com/us-news/article/2024/aug/15/american-jewish-zionism-activism.
43. Shaul Magid, *The Necessity of Exile: Essays from a Distance* (New York: Ayin Press, 2023), 73.
44. Naomi Klein, "We Need an Exodus from Zionism," *The Guardian*, April 24, 2024, https://www.theguardian.com/commentisfree/2024/apr/24/zionism-seder-protest-new-york-gaza-israel.

Chapter 3: Poetry After Genocide

1. Mahmoud Darwish, "*Bitaqah Huwiyya*h / Identity Card," in *Al-A'mal al-Awla / Early Works*, vol. 1, *Awraq Al-Zaytun / Leaves of Olives* (1964) (Beirut: Riad El-Rayyes Books, 2005), 80–84. There are countless translations of this iconic poem of Mahmoud Darwish on and off the internet. This is my own translation from the original Arabic.
2. Theodor Adorno, "Cultural Criticism and Society" (1949), in Theodor W. Adorno, *Prisms*, trans. Samuel Weber and Shierry Weber (Cambridge, MA: MIT Press, 1981), 32–33.
3. Hamid Dabashi, "Gaza: Poetry After Auschwitz," Al Jazeera, August 8, 2014, https://www.aljazeera.com/opinions/2014/8/8/gaza-poetry-after-auschwitz.
4. Klaus Bachmann, *Genocidal Empires: German Colonialism in Africa and the Third Reich* (Berlin: Peter Lang, 2018), 7.
5. Darwish, "*Bitaqah Huwiyyah* / Identity Card."
6. Adorno, "Cultural Criticism and Society," 33.
7. Mahmoud Darwish, *Unfortunately, It Was Paradise: Selected Poems*, trans. and ed. Munir Akash and Carolyn Forché, with Sinan Antoon and Amira El-Zein (Berkeley: University of California Press, 2003), xv.

8. Darwish, *Unfortunately, It Was Paradise*, xv.
9. Darwish, *Unfortunately, It Was Paradise*, xv.
10. Darwish, *Unfortunately, It Was Paradise*, xviii.
11. Samih Shabeeb, "Poetry of Rebellion: The Life, Verse and Death of Nuh Ibrahim During the 1936–39 Revolt," *Jerusalem Quarterly*, no. 25 (Winter 2006): 65.
12. Shabeeb, "Poetry of Rebellion."
13. Darwish, "*Bitaqah Huwiyyah* / Identity Card."
14. Adorno, "Cultural Criticism and Society," 34.
15. Adorno, "Cultural Criticism and Society," 17.
16. Martin Heidegger, "What Are Poets For?" in *Poetry, Language, Thought,* trans. Albert Hofstadter (New York: Harper & Row, 1971), 91.
17. Heidegger, "What Are Poets For?," 242.
18. Darwish, "*Bitaqah Huwiyyah* / Identity Card."
19. Darwish, "*Bitaqah Huwiyyah* / Identity Card."
20. Rasha Khatib, Martin McKee, and Salim Yusuf, "Counting the Dead in Gaza: Difficult but Essential," *The Lancet*, July 10, 2024, https://www.thelancet.com/journals/lancet/article/PIIS0140-6736(24)01169-3/fulltext.
21. Khatib, et al., "Counting the Dead in Gaza."
22. For more on Pontecorvo's life and career, see Carlo Celli, *Gillo Pontecorvo: From Resistance to Terrorism* (Lanham, MD: Scarecrow Press, 2005).
23. Scholars of both Fanon and Pontecorvo have paid attention to this link. See, for example, Haidar Eid and Khaled Ghazel, "Footprints of Fanon in Gillo Pontecorvo's *The Battle of Algiers* and Ousmane Sembene's *Xala*," *English in Africa* 35, no. 2 (October 2008): 151–61, https://www.jstor.org/stable/40239113.
24. For a full report of the Pentagon's attention to the *Battle of Algiers*, see Michael T. Kaufman, "The World: Film Studies;

What Does the Pentagon See in 'Battle of Algiers'?" *The New York Times*, September 7, 2003, https://www.nytimes.com/2003/09/07/weekinreview/the-world-film-studies-what-does-the-pentagon-see-in-battle-of-algiers.html.
25. For a detailed account of the Warsaw Ghetto Uprising, see Dan Kurzman, *The Bravest Battle: The Twenty-Eight Days of the Warsaw Ghetto Uprising* (Boston, MA: Da Capo Press, 1993).
26. Edward Said's documentary is available online at: https://vimeo.com/197028860. Said also published a short essay on Pontecorvo, "The Quest for Gillo Pontecorvo," in *Reflections on Exile and Other Essays* (London: Granta, 2000). For more on this, see Madeleine Dobie, "Edward Said on The Battle of Algiers: The Maghreb, Palestine and Anti-Colonial Aesthetics," *boundary 2*, December 14, 2018, https://www.boundary2.org/2018/12/madeleine-dobie-edward-said-on-the-battle-of-algiers-the-maghreb-palestine-and-anti-colonial-aesthetics/.

Chapter 4: Philosophy After Savagery

1. Immanuel Kant, *Observations on the Feeling of the Beautiful and Sublime*, trans. John T. Goldthwait (Oakland: University of California Press, 1961/2003), 111.
2. Nicole Deitelhoff, Rainer Forst, Klaus Gunther, and Jurgen Habermas, "Principles of Solidarity. A Statement," November 13, 2023, *Normative Orders*, https://www.normativeorders.net/2023/grundsatze-der-solidaritat/.
3. Hamid Dabashi, "Thanks to Gaza, European Philosophy Has Been Exposed as Ethically Bankrupt," *Middle East Eye*, January 18, 2024, https://www.middleeasteye.net/opinion/war-gaza-european-philosophy-ethically-bankrupt-exposed. For the original statement, see Deitelhoff et al., "Principles of Solidarity." For a rebuttal signed by a number of philoso-

phers, see Adam Tooze et al., "The Principle of Human Dignity Must Apply to All People," *The Guardian*, November 22, 2023, https://www.theguardian.com/world/2023/nov/22/the-principle-of-human-dignity-must-apply-to-all-people.

4. Even within the context of European philosophy from which Habermas emerges, he has been the subject of considerable criticism by serious philosophers like Raymond Geuss in his brilliant piece, "A Republic of Discussion: Habermas at Ninety," *Point*, June 18, 2019, https://thepointmag.com/politics/a-republic-of-discussion-habermas-at-ninety/. For further elaborations of this essay, see also Geuss's subsequent piece, "The Last Nineteenth Century German Philosopher: Habermas at 90," *Verso* (blog), August 14, 2019, https://www.versobooks.com/en-gb/blogs/news/4408-the-last-nineteenth-century-german-philosopher-habermas-at-90. For a more detailed account of Geuss's criticism of Habermas, see his pioneering book, *The Idea of a Critical Theory: Habermas and the Frankfurt School* (Cambridge: Cambridge University Press, 1981).

5. "ICJ Says Israel's Presence in Palestinian Territory Is Unlawful," Al Jazeera, July 19, 2024, https://www.aljazeera.com/news/2024/7/19/world-court-says-israels-settlement-policies-breach-international-law.

6. Noa Shpigel, "As Israel's Leaders Seethe at 'Antisemitic' ICJ, Palestinian President Says Justice Has Won," *Haaretz*, July 19, 2024, https://www.haaretz.com/israel-news/2024-07-19/ty-article/.premium/as-israeli-leaders-seethe-at-antisemitic-icj-palestinian-president-says-justice-has-won/00000190-cb67-decf-a7b2-dff7f2240000.

7. Kant, *Observations on the Feeling*, 111.

8. Avram Alpert, "Philosophy's Systemic Racism," Aeon, September 24, 2020, https://aeon.co/essays/racism-is-baked-in-

to-the-structure-of-dialectical-philosophy.
9. Alpert, "Philosophy's Systemic Racism."
10. For more, see Andrew J. Mitchell and Peter Trawny, eds., *Heidegger's Black Notebooks: Responses to Anti-Semitism* (New York: Columbia University Press, 2017).
11. Richard Wolin, *The Politics of Being: The Political Thought of Martin Heidegger* (New York: Columbia University Press, 2016).
12. Daniel James and Franz Knappik, "Exploring the Metaphysics of Hegel's Racism: The Teleology of the 'Concept' and the Taxonomy of Races," in "Hegel and Teleology," special issue, *Hegel Bulletin* 44 (2023): 99–126.
13. James and Knappik, "Exploring the Metaphysics."
14. James and Knappik, "Exploring the Metaphysics."
15. Sandra Bonetto, "Race and Racism in Hegel—An Analysis," *Minerva: An Internet Journal of Philosophy* 10 (2006): 35–64 at 35, http://www.minerva.mic.ul.ie/vol10/Hegel.pdf.
16. Bonetto, "Race and Racism in Hegel," 37.
17. See Elzbieta Ettinger, *Hannah Arendt / Martin Heidegger* (New Haven, CT: Yale University Press, 1997).
18. Darrel Moellendorf, "Racism and Rationality in Hegel's Philosophy of Subjective Sprit," *History of Political Thought* 13, no. 2 (Summer 1992): 243–255, at 243.
19. Moellendorf, "Racism and Rationality," 247.
20. For just one example of critical takes on what has rightly been called a "genocide" of Native Americans, see Maka Monture Paki, "American Genocide: The Crimes of Native American Boarding Schools Embarks on a Quest for Truth and Healing," *Vanity Fair*, May 10, 2023, https://www.vanityfair.com/style/2023/05/american-genocide-the-crimes-of-native-american-boarding-schools-truth-and-healing.
21. Jong Seok Na, "The Dark Side of Hegel's Theory of Modernity: Race and the Other," *Esercizi Filosofici* 14 (2019): 49–71,

at 1, https://www.openstarts.units.it/server/api/core/bitstreams/93e3e763-886e-45e9-8267-73d410101fd5/content.
22. Na, "Dark Side of Hegel's Theory," 1.
23. Na, "Dark Side of Hegel's Theory," 69.
24. See Michael O. Hardimon, "Where Did Hegel Go Wrong on Race?" *Hegel Bulletin* 95 (2024), *Hegel Bulletin* 45 (2024): 23–42.
25. Robert Bernasconi, "Will the Real Kant Please Stand Up: The Challenge of Enlightenment Racism to the Study of the History of Philosophy," *Radical Philosophy* 117 (January/February 2003): 13–22, at 13, https://www.radicalphilosophy.com/article/will-the-real-kant-please-stand-up.
26. Bernasconi, "Will the Real Kant Please Stand Up," 14.
27. Bernasconi, "Will the Real Kant Please Stand Up," 15.
28. Bernasconi, "Will the Real Kant Please Stand Up," 16. For yet another futile attempt to save Hegel's racist philosophy from critical judgment, see Joseph McCarney's "Hegel's Racism? A Response to Bernasconi," *Radical Philosophy* 119 (May/June 2003): 32–35, https://www.radicalphilosophy.com/extras/mccarney-hegels-racism.
29. Enrique Dussel, *Philosophy of Liberation* (New York: Orbis Books, 1980), 3.
30. All these and other such phrases and sentiments are cited and discussed by Robert Eaglestone in his essay "Postcolonial Thought and Levinas's Double Vision," in *Radicalizing Levinas*, ed. Peter Atterton and Matthew Calarco (Albany, NY: State University of New York Press, 2010): 57–68.
31. See Raja Abdulrahim, "Stripped, Beaten or Vanished: Israel's Treatment of Gaza Detainees Raises Alarm," *The New York Times*, January 23, 2024, https://www.nytimes.com/2024/01/23/world/middleeast/israel-gaza-palestinian-detainees.html.

32. Abdulrahim, "Stripped, Beaten or Vanished."
33. CNN International Investigations and Visuals Team, "Strapped Down, Blindfolded, Held in Diapers: Israeli Whistleblowers Detail Abuse of Palestinians in Shadowy Detention Center," CNN, May 11, 2024, https://www.cnn.com/2024/05/10/middleeast/israel-sde-teiman-detention-whistleblowers-intl-cmd/index.html.
34. Dussel, *Philosophy of Liberation*, 4.
35. United Nations, Office of the High Commissioner for Human Rights, "Israel/oPt: UN Experts Appalled by Reported Human Rights Violations Against Palestinian Women and Girls," press release, February 19, 2024, https://www.ohchr.org/en/press-releases/2024/02/israelopt-un-experts-appalled-reported-human-rights-violations-against.

Chapter 5: The Garrison State Versus the Palestinian Camp

1. Tracy Smith, "Children of Gaza," CBS News, *Sunday Morning*, July 21, 2024, https://www.cbsnews.com/news/children-of-gaza/.
2. Lazar Berman, "After Walling Itself In, Israel Learns to Hazard the Jungle Beyond," *Times of Israel*, March 8, 2021, https://www.timesofisrael.com/after-walling-itself-in-israel-learns-to-hazard-the-jungle-beyond/.
3. Smith, "Children of Gaza."
4. Harold D. Lasswell, "The Garrison State," *American Journal of Sociology* 46, no. 4 (January 1941): 455–68, at 455.
5. "President Dwight D. Eisenhower's Farewell Address (1961)," National Archives, https://www.archives.gov/milestone-documents/president-dwight-d-eisenhowers-farewell-address. To watch President Eisenhower deliver the

speech with some historical commentary, see US National Archives, "Eisenhower's 'Military-Industrial Complex' Speech Origins and Significance," YouTube, January 19, 2011, https://www.youtube.com/watch?v=Gg-jvHynP9Y.
6. Lasswell, "The Garrison State," 459.
7. Lasswell, "The Garrison State," 462–63.
8. Lasswell, "The Garrison State," 463.
9. Aaron L. Friedberg, *In the Shadow of the Garrison State: America's Anti-Statism and Its Cold War Grand Strategy* (Princeton, NJ: Princeton University Press, 2000).
10. For more on Project 2025, prepared by the reactionary outlet Heritage Foundation as a blueprint for the second term of Donald Trump's presidency, see Simon J. Levien, "What Is Project 2025, and Why Is Trump Disavowing It?" *The New York Times*, July 11, 2024, https://www.nytimes.com/article/project-2025.html.
11. Milton J. Esman, "Toward the American Garrison State," *Peace Review: A Journal of Social Justice* 19, no. 3 (2007): 407–16, https://doi.org/10.1080/10402650701525003.
12. Dwight J. Simpson, "Israel: A Garrison State," *Current History* 58, no. 341, (1970): 1–47, at 1.
13. Simpson, "Israel: A Garrison State," 3.
14. Steve Goldfield, *Garrison State: Israel's Role in U.S. Global Strategy* (San Francisco, CA: Palestine Focus Publications, 1985).
15. Seymour M. Hersh, "The Traitor," *The New Yorker*, January 10, 1999, https://www.newyorker.com/magazine/1999/01/18/the-traitor.
16. I first developed this idea in a short essay, "ISIL as Total State and Pure Violence," Al Jazeera, July 24, 2016, https://www.aljazeera.com/opinions/2016/7/24/isil-as-total-state-and-pure-violence.

17. I first outlined this argument in an essay, "The End of the Nation-State," Al Jazeera, January 25, 2020, https://www.aljazeera.com/opinions/2020/1/25/the-end-of-the-nation-state. I subsequently developed the idea further in *The Emperor Is Naked: On the Inevitable Demise of the Nation-State* (London: Zed Books, 2020).
18. Giorgio Agamben, *Remnants of Auschwitz: The Witness and the Archive* (New York: Zone Books, 1999), 41.
19. Giorgio Agamben, *Means Without End: Notes on Politics* (University of Minnesota Press, 2000), 24. For a documentary film on these deported Palestinians, see Bahea Namoor, "Palestinians Displaced by Force," Al Jazeera, Palestine Remix, 2014, https://remix.aljazeera.com/aje/PalestineRemix/deportees.html#/21. "On a cold December day in 1992," you read here, "415 Palestinians from the OPT were expelled to South Lebanon, after deportation orders were issued in the West Bank and Gaza Strip without any prior notice to the families. Deportees were handcuffed and blindfolded, and put in buses to be driven to South Lebanon."
20. Giorgio Agamben, *Means Without End: Notes on Politics*, trans. Vincenzo Binetti and Cesare Casarino (Minneapolis: University of Minnesota Press, 1996), 24–25.
21. Agamben, *Remnants of Auschwitz*, 45.
22. Agamben, *Remnants of Auschwitz*, 45.
23. Agamben, *Remnants of Auschwitz*, 45.
24. Jean Améry, *At the Mind's Limits: Contemplations by a Survivor on Auschwitz and Its Realities*, trans. Sidney Rosenfeld and Stella P. Rosenfeld (Bloomington: Indiana University Press, 1980), 9, quoted in Agamben, *Remnants of Auschwitz*, 41.
25. Giorgio Agamben, *Homo Sacer: Sovereign Power and Bare Life*, trans. Daniel Heller-Roazen (Stanford, CA: Stanford University Press, 1998), 188–89.

26. Agamben, *Homo Sacer*, 95.
27. Agamben, *Homo Sacer*, 96–97.
28. Agamben, *Homo Sacer*, 96.
29. See "The Nakba Did Not Start or End in 1948," Al Jazeera, May 23, 2017, https://www.aljazeera.com/features/2017/5/23/the-nakba-did-not-start-or-end-in-1948.
30. Agamben, *Homo Sacer*, 97.
31. Agamben, *Homo Sacer*, 99.
32. Aldo Carpi, *Diario di Gusen* (Turin: Einaudi, 1993), 17, quoted in Agamben, *Remnants of Auschwitz*, 41.
33. Nurhan Abujidi, "The Palestinian States of Exception and Agamben," *Contemporary Arab Affairs* 2, no. 2 (2009): 272–91, https://doi.org/10.1080/17550910902857034.
34. United Nations, High Commissioner for Refugees, "Refugee Statistics," https://www.unrefugees.org/refugee-facts/statistics/.
35. Michel Agier, *Managing the Undesirables: Refugee Camps and Humanitarian Government*, trans. David Fernbach (Cambridge, UK: Polity Press, 2010).
36. Leonardo Schiocchet, "Palestinian Refugees in Lebanon: Is the Camp a Space of Exception?," *Mashriq and Mahjar* 2, no. 1 (2014): 142–74, https://doi.org/10.24847/22i2014.29.
37. Zdzisław Ryn and Stanisław Kłodziński, "An der Grenze zwischen Leben und Tod: Eine Studie über die Erscheinung des 'Muselmanns' im Konzentrationslager," in Hamburger Institut für Sozialforschung (ed.), Die Auschwitz-Hefte - Band I (Weinheim and Basel: Beltz Verlag, 1987), 89–154, at 128-29, quoted in Agamben, *Remnants of Auschwitz*, 42, https://www.mp.pl/auschwitz/journal/german/176576,die-auschwitz-hefte-band-1

Chapter 6: Palestine Beyond Borders

1. "Resignation Letter of Craig Mokhiber, Director in the New York Office of the United Nations High Commissioner for Human Rights," L'Art Rue, October 28, 2023, https://lartrue.org/en/resignation-letter-of-craig-mokhiber-director-in-the-new-york-office-of-the-high-commissioner-for-human-rights. For more details on this resignation letter, see Ed Pilkington, "Top UN Official in New York Steps Down Citing 'Genocide' of Palestinian Civilians," *The Guardian*, October 31, 2023, https://www.theguardian.com/world/2023/oct/31/un-official-resigns-israel-hamas-war-palestine-new-york. For a conversation with Craig Mokhiber about Palestinian genocide, see "Q&A: Former UN Official Craig Mokhiber on Gaza, Israel and Genocide," Al Jazeera, November 2, 2023, https://www.aljazeera.com/amp/news/2023/11/2/qa-former-un-official-craig-mokhiber-on-gaza-and-genocide.
2. Samuel Huntington, *The Clash of Civilizations and the Remaking of World Order* (New York: Simon and Schuster, 2011).
3. Hamid Dabashi, "For the Last Time: Civilizations," *International Journal of Sociology* 16, no. 3 (2001), https://doi.org/10.1177/026858001016003.
4. I have detailed this argument in *The End of Two Illusions: Islam After the West* (Oakland: University of California Press, 2022).
5. See AJLabs, "What Countries Has Israel Attacked Since October 7?" Al Jazeera, August 1, 2024, https://www.aljazeera.com/news/2024/8/1/what-countries-has-israel-attacked-since-october-7.
6. "Resignation Letter of Craig Mokhiber."
7. The first version of this part of this final chapter was

published as an afterword to a special issue of *South Atlantic Quarterly* 117, no. 1 (January 2018), "Palestine Beyond National Frames: Emerging Politics, Cultures, and Claims." In that afterword, I was obviously referring to the collection of essays in that volume. I have dispensed with those references in this chapter. But I strongly recommend the volume as a fine sample of collective and collaborative scholarship on a singularly significant aspect of Palestinian polity. I am grateful to Sophie Richter-Devroe and Rubah Salih, the guest editors of the issue, for their kind invitation to write that afterword.

8. For more, see Marek Edelman, *The Ghetto Fights: Warsaw 1941–43* (London: Turnaround, 1990).

9. Amos Goldberg, "Yes, It Is Genocide," trans. Sol Salbe, Medium, April 18, 2024, https://thepalestineproject.medium.com/yes-it-is-genocide-634a07ea27d4. For a subsequent interview with Professor Goldberg, see Elias Feroz, "Israeli Historian: This Is Exactly What Genocide Looks Like," *Jacobin*, July 11, 2024, https://jacobin.com/2024/07/amos-goldberg-genocide-gaza-israel.

10. "Resignation Letter of Craig Mokhiber."

11. In my book *Iran Without Borders: Towards a Critique of the Postcolonial Nation* (London and New York: Verso, 2016), I offered a detailed account of how the making of the postcolonial nation was already transnational, meaning it was predicated on the formation of the idea of the nation on a transnational public sphere that extended from its European bourgeois side and moved all the way to its colonial extensions.

12. Rachel Cooke, "Emily Jacir: Europa Review—This Is Art as a Cause," *The Guardian*, October 4, 2015, https://www.theguardian.com/artanddesign/2015/oct/04/emily-jacir-europa-whitechapel-gallery-review-one-sided-message.

13. Cooke, "Emily Jacir."
14. Cooke, "Emily Jacir."
15. "Resignation Letter of Craig Mokhiber."
16. Emily Genauer, *Marc Chagall* (New York: Harvey N. Abrams, 1956), plate 15.

Conclusion: Writing at the Time of a Genocide

1. James Baldwin, "Open Letter to the Born Again," *The Nation*, September 29, 1979, https://www.thenation.com/article/society/open-letter-born-again/.
2. Ahmet Gurhan Kartal, "What We Are Seeing in Gaza Is a 'Repeat of Auschwitz,' Says Genocide Expert," Anadolu Ajansi, April 29, 2024, https://www.aa.com.tr/en/middle-east/what-we-are-seeing-in-gaza-is-a-repeat-of-auschwitz-says-genocide-expert/3202869.
3. Baldwin, "Open Letter to the Born Again."
4. Shaul Magid, *The Necessity of Exile: Essays from a Distance* (New York: Ayin Press, 2023). Other leading Jewish thinkers have been meditating on similar ideas. In his compelling argument in *The No-State Solution: A Jewish Manifesto* (New Haven, CT: Yale University Press, 2023), Daniel Boyarin has also put forward a similar post-Zionist argument by separating the idea of nation and state. In June 2024, there was a major conference in Berlin addressing similar ideas of exilic Judaism in which the leading scholars of the field had participated. The Israeli liberal Zionist outfit *Haaretz* covered this conference with a sarcastic and dismissive tone, ridiculing the assumption that scholars like Magid and Boyarin are US Jews and clueless about the practicalities of their ideas. See Ofri Ilani, "Zero States for Two Peoples? Jewish Thinkers Are Pondering a Mass Return to Exile," *Haaretz*, August 9,

2024, https://www.haaretz.com/israel-news/2024-08-09/ty-article-opinion/.highlight/zero-states-for-two-peoples-jewish-scholars-are-pondering-a-mass-return-to-exile/00000191-3327-dddb-abb5-73f74bb90000.
5. Magid, *Necessity of Exile*, 73.
6. Magid, *Necessity of Exile*, 42.
7. Magid, *Necessity of Exile*, 224.
8. Magid, *Necessity of Exile*, 227.
9. For a potent critic of Edward Said's secularism as concealed Christianity, see Gil Anidjar, "Secularism," *Critical Inquiry* 33, no. 1 (Autumn 2006): 52–77.
10. Edward Said, *Representations of the Intellectual* (New York: Vintage Books, 1996), 52–53, https://doi.org/10.1086/509746.
11. Said, *Representations of the Intellectual*, 33.
12. Said, *Representations of the Intellectual*, 33.
13. We, of course, know that, during an interview with *Haaretz*, Said in fact considered himself "the last Jewish intellectual." For more details on Said's relationship with Judaism, see Joseph Massad, "The Intellectual Life of Edward Said," *Journal of Palestine Studies* 33, no. 3 (Spring 2004): 7–22, https://doi.org/10.1525/jps.2004.33.3.007.
14. Hamid Dabashi, *Remembrance of Things Past: On Edward Said* (Chicago: Haymarket Books, 2020), 89–105.
15. In my more recent work, I have developed the idea of "pilgrim" and "nomad" as a more appropriate designation of how we live our lives on this earth. See Hamid Dabashi, "The Nomadic Fate of the Persian Prince," chap. eight in *The Persian Prince: The Rise and Resurrection of an Imperial Archetype*, (Stanford, CA: Stanford University Press, 2022).
16. Baldwin, "Open Letter to the Born Again."
17. Mahmoud Darwish, "*Bitaqah Huwiyyah* / Identity Card,"

in *Al-A'mal al-Awla / Early Works, vol. 1, Awraq Al-Zaytun / Leaves of Olives* (1964) (Beirut: Riad El-Rayyes Books, 2005).

18. Maulana Jalal al-Din Balkhi, "Ghazal 648," in *Kolyyat-e Shams: Divan-e Kabir*, ed. Badi' al-Zaman Forouzanfar, vol. 2 (Tehran: Amir Kabir, 1958), 65.

Index

Page numbers followed by "n" denote notes.

absolute reification, 67–68
Abu Akleh, Shireen, 50
Abujidi, Nurhan, 129
Adorno, Theodor, xviii, 42–46; "Cultural Criticism and Society," 62–63; evolution of critical perspective on, 59–60; geographic and cultural limitations of Adorno's perspective, 62–63; position, contextual legitimacy of, 76–77
Agamben, Giorgio, xix, xxvii, 128; on bare life of camp's inhabitants, 126; camp as biopolitical paradigm, 123–24; camp as space of exception, 124–25; critique of his European limitations, 119–21; *Homo Sacer: Sovereign Power and Bare Life,* 123; idea of "the camp," 105–6; *Means Without End: Notes on Politics,* 116; *Remnants of Auschwitz: The Witness and the Archive,* xix, 116, 118, 122, 128; theory of the camp as modern sovereignty, 115, 116–18
Agier, Michel, 130; *Managing the Undesirables: Refugee Camps and Humanitarian Government,* 130
Ajami, Fouad, 164
Albanese, Francesca, 41, 49
al-Ali, Naji, xix
Allen, Amy, 48; *The End of*

Progress: Decolonizing the Normative Foundations of Critical Theory, 48
Alpert, Avram, 85–86; *Partial Enlightenment: What Modern Literature and Buddhism Can Teach Us About Living Well Without Perfection*, 85; "Philosophy's Systemic Racism," 85
Améry, Jean, 122
Amichai, Yehuda, 65
amphibian vs. exilic intellectuals, 164–65
anthropological gaze, 100
anthropological reading of European philosophy, 96–98
appropriation of universal heritage, 97
Arab Revolt, 125–26
Arendt, Hannah, 90, 117
Armed Conflict Location and Event Data Project (ACLED), 136

Bachmann, Klaus, 60–61; *Genocidal Empires: German Colonialism in Africa and the Third Reich*, 60–61
Baldwin, James, 153, 154, 157, 158, 167
Balfour Declaration, 117
barbarism: alternative literary traditions as response to, 70–71; colonial double standard of, 68–69; metaphysics of, xxvii–xxix; poetry after genocide as civilizational affirmation against, 73–77; poetry as transcendence vs., 71–72
bare life, 126, 130
The Battle of Algiers / La battaglia di Algeri (film), 73–74
BDS (Boycott, Divestment, Sanctions) movement, 140–41
Beinart, Peter, 53, 55–56
being Palestinian, 17
Bellah, Robert, 51
belonging, conception of, 165
Benvenisti, Meron, 37
Bernasconi, Robert, 93–95
Black Notebooks (Heidegger), 86
Black Skin, White Masks (Fanon), 74
Bonetto, Sandra, 88
Boyarin, Daniel, 201n4; *The No-State Solution: A Jewish Manifesto*, 201n4

INDEX

Braidotti, Rosi, 101; *Posthuman Knowledge*, 101
Brennan, Timothy, 3; *Places of Mind: A Life of Edward Said*, 3
British colonialism, xxvi, 66
Brown Skin, White Masks, 164, 165
Burj el-Barajneh Camp, 21
Bush, George W., 111

camps: bare life of inhabitants, 126; as biopolitical paradigm, 123–24; colonial precedence to European, 122–24; as contested space, 130–31; idea of "the camp," 105–6; law/fact indistinguishability in, 126–27; as modern sovereignty, theory of the, 115, 116–18; Palestinian camps as the site of colonial modernity, 122–28; as space of exception, 124–25
capitalist modernity, xxv, 48, 76, 106, 122–23, 128, 129, 155
Carpi, A., 128
Cavafy, C. P., 65
Césaire, Aimé, xvi

Chagall, Marc, 150–51
civic protections, 115
civil disobedience, 147
civilizational thinking, 135–36
civil religion, 51–52
"clash of civilizations" framework, critique of, 135–36
cognitive dissonance as emancipatory force, 147
collective consciousness, 51–52
collective suffering, 52
colonial complicity, Frankfurt School's, 41–49
colonial continuity, 121
colonial double standard of "barbarism," 68–69
colonial expansion and dispossession, 32–34
colonial gaze, 88
colonial genocide as historical norm, 61
coloniality: and global conception of "the West and the Rest," 10–11; and idea of "the World," 8
colonial modernity, 118, 121–22; Palestinian camps as the site of, 122–28, 136, 138
colonial precedence to European camps, 122–24
colonial racism, 91–92

colonial reality, deliberate concealment of, 35
colonial violence: effect of, 127–28; historical examples, 124; as invisible norm, 68–71; in Palestinian poetry, 65–66
colonial vs. settler-colonial formations, 36
The Concept of the Political (Schmitt), 105
confirmation bias, 87
Conrad, Joseph, xiv; *Heart of Darkness*, xiv, 40
counter-Zionism, 56–57; as ethical alternative, 158–61, 164–65
critical agency, 69–70
critical complicity, 76–77
critical intelligence, 68
critical thinking, 93, 143–44, 171
cultural criticism, 62, 67, 69–71
"Cultural Criticism and Society" (Adorno), 62–63
cultural critics, 76
cultural racism, 91
culture of resistance vs. culture of conquest, 13

Damrosch, David, 6

Dana, Tariq, 36
The Darker Side of Western Modernity: Global Futures, Decolonial Options (Mignolo), 70
Darwish, Mahmoud, 26–29, 59, 67, 72, 73, 172; as counterexample of Adorno's perspective, 62, 64–66
decoloniality, 11–12; and postcoloniality, 9–10
decolonizing philosophy, 88
dehumanization: and "bare life," 130; logic of Western philosophy, 82; philosophical calamity of, 97–98
Deitelhoff, Nicole, 80
de las Casas, Bartolome, 52
deuniversalization and death of the West, 168–69
Dialectic of Enlightenment (Horkheimer), 70
"dictatorial," 110
dispossession, 32, 37–38, 106, 115, 129–30, 188n42
divine presence in suffering, 172–74
Durkheim, Émile, 51
Dussel, Enrique, 47, 96, 99
Dying Colonialism (Fanon), 74

Edelman, Marek, 138–39
Eisenhower, Dwight D., 108–9
Elhalaby, Esmat, 3
Emmanuel, Arghiri, 35
Encyclopedia Judaica, 119–20
The End of Progress: Decolonizing the Normative Foundations of Critical Theory (Allen), 48
Enlightenment modernity, 70, 71, 168
epistemic limitations of European theory, 121
epistemological challenge to "world" concepts, 5–6
epistemological rupture, 99–101
Esman, Milton J., 111
The Ethnic Cleansing of Palestine (Pappé), 33
ethnocentrism, 56, 89–90, 159
ethnophilosophy trap, 95
Eurocentric Christianity, 91
Eurocentric Critical Theory: critique of, 60; failure of, 41–49; limitations of, 59–61; myopic nature of, 65–66
Eurocentric imagination, 73, 99
European appropriation of the Greeks, 97
European colonial anxiety and paralysis, 150
European colonialism, xv, xxii, 29, 34, 42, 66, 85, 87, 141, 150, 168
European critical self-implication, paradox of, 67–69
European identity through othering, 120–21
European Islamophobia and antisemitism, 119–20
European philosophy: anthropological reading of, 96–98; blind spots of, 123–24; moral philosophy, 83; racism in, 79–81, 84–95. *See also* Western philosophy
European provincialism, 93
European racist imagination, 117
European universalism, 92–93
Evangelical Zionism, 5, 51, 52
exile as liberating theological concept, 158–65
"Exterminate All the Brutes" (Lindqvist), xiv, 40
external Others, xvii, 55, 81, 120, 121

Fanon, Frantz, 74, 92; *Black Skin, White Masks,* 74;

Dying Colonialism, 74; *The Wretched of the Earth*, 74
Faye, Emmanuel, 86; *Heidegger: The Introduction of Nazism into Philosophy in Light of the Unpublished Seminars of 1933–1935*, 86
Fertile Memory (film), 18
folk poetry as resistance, 65
Forst, Rainer, 80
Friedberg, Aaron L., 110–11; *In the Shadow of the Garrison State: America's Anti-Statism and Its Cold War Grand Strategy*, 110–11
Frye, Northrop, 105; *Literary History of Canada*, 105

Gallant, Yoav, xix
garrison mentality, 105
garrison state, characteristic of, 105–6
Garrison State: Israel's Role in U.S. Global Strategy (Goldfield), 113–14
garrison state versus the Palestinian camp: garrison state, characteristics of, 105–6; Israeli garrison state, 107–15; Israeli garrison state and the Palestinian camps, 128–32; Muselmann: from the Jewish to the Palestinian camp, 115–22; Palestinian camps as the site of (colonial) modernity, 122–28
Gaza: genocide as historical turning point, 167–71; as metaphor and new epistemic center, 169; as new metaphysical foundation, 83; space of exception, 125
Genauer, Emily, 151; *The Praying Jew*, 151
genealogy of genocidal practices, 33–34
Genocidal Empires: German Colonialism in Africa and the Third Reich (Bachmann), 60–61
genocidal Zionism, xvii, 14, 84, 134, 168
genocide: colonial genocide as historical norm, 61; Gaza genocide as historical turning point, 167–71; global recognition of, 142; Herero and Nama genocide, 34; Libyan, 121; political paralysis after the Palestinian, 101–2. *See also* poetry

German colonialism, 60–61
Ghassan Kanafani Cultural Foundation, 16, 21
globalized capitalism, 38, 39–40, 136, 141, 155
global refugee crisis as planetary condition, 129–30
Goldberg, Amos, 142
Goldfield, Steve, 113–14; *Garrison State: Israel's Role in U.S. Global Strategy*, 113–14
"Governmentalized," 109
Günther, Klaus, 80
Gutierrez, Gustavo, 52

Haaretz, 201n4
Habermas, Jürgen, xix, 80
Haniqra, Rosh, 37
Hardimon, Michael O., 93
Heart of Darkness (Conrad), xiv, 40
Hegel, Georg Wilhelm Friedrich, 90; *Philosophy of History*, 90; *Philosophy of Subjective Spirit*, 93; racist spirit, phenomenology of, 84–95
Heidegger, Martin, 71–72, 86; *Black Notebooks*, 86
Heidegger: The Introduction of Nazism into Philosophy in Light of the Unpublished Seminars of 1933–1935 (Faye), 86
Heidegger and Nazism (Farias), 96
Herero and Nama genocide, 34
Hersh, Seymour M., 114; *The Samson Option: Israel's Nuclear Arsenal and American Foreign Policy*, 114
Herzl, Theodor, 33, 37
Herzog, Isaac, xxii–xxiv
Hölderlin, 71–72
Homo Sacer: Sovereign Power and Bare Life (Agamben), 123
"homo sacer," 115
Horkheimer, Max, 42–46, 70; *Dialectic of Enlightenment*, 70
Horowitz, David, 165
How the World Made the West: A 4,000 Year History (Quinn), 135–36
humanitarian crisis, xxiii, 98, 127, 130, 134
Huntington, Samuel, 135, 136

Ibrahim, Nuh, 65
identity: European identity through othering, 120–21; national, 139. *See*

also Palestinian identity
ideological justification
through "better use,"
37–38
implicated criticism, paradox
of, 67–68
institutional critique, 101
institutional memory and
commemoration, 33
intercultural dialogues, 92
interlocutor, shifting the,
99–101
internal Others, xvii, 55, 81,
120, 121
International Court of Justice,
84
*In the Shadow of the Garrison
State: America's Anti-Statism and Its Cold War
Grand Strategy* (Friedberg), 110–11
Iranophobia, 145
*Iran Without Borders: Towards
a Critique of the Postcolonial Nation* (Dabashi),
200n11
Isaac, Munther, Reverend,
50–51, 53
Isfahani, Hatef, 159
Islamic prayer rituals, 120
Islamophobia: and antisemitism, 119–20; Western,
145. *See also* "Muselmann"
and colonial connections
Israel: as imperial extension
of capital, 136–37; Israeli
garrison state, 107–15;
Israeli garrison state and
the Palestinian camps,
128–32. *See also* Zionism

Jacir, Emily, 144–46
James, Daniel, 87
Jarbawi, Ali, 36
Jeffries, Stuart, 43
Jewish exile, 161
Jewish liberation theology,
54, 57

Kanafani, Anni, 15–16, 20,
22–24
Kanafani, Ghassan, 15–16, 20–
24; "Al-Qandil al-Saghir /
The Little Lantern," 20–21
Kant, Immanuel, xxvii–xxix,
80, 84, 95; *Observations on
the Feeling of the Beautiful
and Sublime*, xxix
Khleifi, Michel, 18
Kipling, Rudyard, 68
Klein, Naomi, 57
Knappik, Franz, 87
knowledge production, 5–6,
8–9, 171; after Gaza,

99–101; imperial, 12
Kulturkritik (cultural critic), 69–70

language, 63, 118–19
Lasswell, Harold D., 106, 108–11
Latin American liberation theology, 91
Levinas, Emmanuel, 96–98
liberation theology, Palestinian, 50–53
Libyan genocide, 121
Lindqvist, Sven, xiv, 40; *"Exterminate All the Brutes,"* xiv, 40
Literary History of Canada (Frye), 105
literary traditions as response to barbarism, alternative, 70–71
The Little Lantern (Rizzi), 17, 18–24
Lloyd, David, 38
Lorca, Federico Garcia, 65

Magid, Shaul, 56–57, 158–61, 163, 165; *The Necessity of Exile: Essays from a Distance*, 158
Managing the Undesirables: Refugee Camps and Humanitarian Government (Agier), 130
Mandela, Nelson, 54–55
Mandelstam, Osip, 65
Mar Elias refugee camp, 16
Means Without End: Notes on Politics (Agamben), 116
Meir, Golda, 13
metaphysics of barbarism, xxvii–xxix
Mignolo, Walter, 70; *The Darker Side of Western Modernity: Global Futures, Decolonial Options*, 70
military-industrial complex, 108–9
Moellendorf, Darrel, 90
Mokhiber, Craig, 134, 138, 143, 149
moral authority, xxi, xxvi, 134, 138, 169
moral imagination, 53, 81
moral legitimacy, 115
"Muselmann" and colonial connections, 115–22. See also Islamophobia
Muselmänner, 116, 120

Na, Jong Seok, 91–92
Nakba/Catastrophe, 9, 11, 21–22, 66, 80, 104, 139, 140

national consciousness, 17, 140, 142, 145, 149
national identity, 139
nation-state as colonial construct, 138
Nazi concentration camps, 117–18
The Necessity of Exile: Essays from a Distance (Magid), 158
Neruda, Pablo, 65
Neshat, Shirin, 18, 145
Netanyahu, Benjamin, 82–83
The No-State Solution: A Jewish Manifesto (Boyarin), 201n4

Observations on the Feeling of the Beautiful and Sublime (Kant), xxix
The Order of Terror: The Concentration Camp (Sofsky), 118–19
Orientalism (Said), 9–10, 101
orientalist vocabulary in Critical Theory, 44
orientalizing language across camps, 118–19
othering, European identity through, 81, 120–21; external Others, xvii, 55, 81, 120, 121; internal Others, xvii, 55, 81, 120, 121
Out of Place (Said), 9

Palestine: as active knowledge producer, 5–6, 8–9; as decolonial completion, 9–10; as epistemological challenge, 8–10; as global metaphor and repository, 11–14; as a political question of settler colonialism, 4–6; as semiotic force field, 14–15; as a site of contestation, 10–14; as universal liberation struggle, 134–35
Palestinian: cinema, 17–19; exceptionalism vs. universal theory, 129–32; idea of a, 25–30; vs. Jewish European artists, 149–51; Jews, 4–5, 12–13; liberation theology, 50–53; national liberation and transnational solidarity, 138–42; pluralism vs. genocidal ideology, 14; resistance as structural obstacle, 36–37; states of exception, 129
Palestinian identity: artistic identity, double bind of,

143–47; erasure of, 43; expanded definition of, 15–16; as transnational phenomenon, 17–18; as universal human condition, 169

Palestinian poetry: as challenge to European frameworks, 61–62; as universal rather than provincial, 64–66; universal significance of, 72

Pappé, Ilan, 2, 32–33, 38–39; *The Ethnic Cleansing of Palestine,* 33

Parsipur, Shahrnush, 18

Partial Enlightenment: What Modern Literature and Buddhism Can Teach Us About Living Well Without Perfection (Alpert), 85

phenomenology of Hegel's racist spirit, 84–95

philosophical calamity of dehumanization, 97–98

philosophical intelligence, 99

philosophical racism, European, 79–81, 84–95

Philosophy of History (Hegel), 90

Philosophy of Subjective Spirit (Hegel), 93

"Philosophy's Systemic Racism" (Alpert), 85

"philosophy" term: containing to Europe, 95; monopolization of, 82

Pipes, Daniel, 165

Places of Mind: A Life of Edward Said (Brennan), 3

poetic intuition of transcendence, 71

poetry: after genocide as civilizational affirmation against barbarism, 73–77; folk, 65; as necessary response to barbarism in non-European traditions, 70–71; Palestinian poetry as challenge to European frameworks, 61–62; Palestinian poetry as universal rather than provincial, 64–66; as transcendence vs. barbarism, 71–72; universal significance of Palestinian poetry, 72

political analysis of European philosophy, need for, 96–98

political paralysis after the Palestinian genocide, 101–2

The Politics of Being (Wolin), 86

Pollard, Jonathan Jay, 114

Pontecorvo, Gillo, 73–74
postcolonial imagination, 138
Posthuman Knowledge (Braidotti), 101
post-Islamist liberation theology, 174
post-Islamist state of thinking and being, 164
Post-Orientalism (Said), 101
post-Western world order, 137
post-Zionist Jewish liberation theology, 174
The Praying Jew (Genauer), 151
predatory capitalism, 131

"Al-Qandil al-Saghir / The Little Lantern" (Kanafani), 20–21
The Question of Palestine (Said), 56
Quinn, Josephine, 135–36; *How the World Made the West: A 4,000 Year History,* 135–36

race's biological status, 93
racism: colonial, 91–92; European philosophical, 79–81, 84–95; racialized gaze, 88; racialized language and double standards, 42–43; racist delusion, 55

regional destabilization, 136–37
reified ideology, 68
religious conversion, 91
religious nationalism, critique of, 141
Remnants of Auschwitz: The Witness and the Archive (Agamben), xix, 116, 118, 122, 128
renegade text, 9–10
Representations of the Intellectual (Said), 164
Rilke, Rainer Maria, 72
Rizzi, Mario, 16–18, 19–20, 21–24, 25–30; *The Little Lantern,* 17, 18–24
Rockhill, Gabriel, 42, 43–44, 46
Rodinson, Maxime, 35
Rousseau, Jean-Jacques, 85–86
Royal African Company, 94

Said, Edward, 2, 3–4, 9–10, 25, 56, 75–76, 101, 161–65; *Orientalism,* 9–10, 101; *Out of Place,* 9; *Post-Orientalism,* 101; *The Question of Palestine,* 56; *Representations of the Intellectual,* 164
The Samson Option: Israel's Nuclear Arsenal and

American Foreign Policy (Hersh), 114
Schiller, Friedrich, 85
Schiocchet, Leonardo, 130–31
Schmitt, Carl, 105; *The Concept of the Political,* 105
settler-colonial: Christianity, 52; demographics, 32–34; mentality, 105; normalization project, 127–28; understanding the term, 117; violence, 61. *See also* colonial violence
settler colonialism: defined, 35–36; erasure of the natives, 37–38; as impermanence and instability, 11; scholarly recognition of, 36–40
Shagar, Rav, 161
Shāhid, xix
Shatz, Adam, 3
Simpson, Dwight J., 112–13
Sirhan, Ibrahim Hassan, 17–18
Smith, Tracy, 104, 108
Sofsky, Wolfgang, 118–19; *The Order of Terror: The Concentration Camp,* 118–19
Sontag, Susan, 3
state: as an entity, 115; of exception, 131; theology, defined, 49–50
Suez Canal Crisis, 5
systematic elimination and replacement logic, 35

"tabloid philosophy," 96
transcending Western validation, 150–51
transnational consciousness as authentically Palestinian, 143–44
transnational solidarity, Palestinian national liberation and, 138–42
tribalism, 87, 89–90, 157, 168

universalism, 92–93
universality through military power, false, 83

Vázquez-Arroyo, Antonio Y., 47
Veracini, Lorenzo, 36

War on Terror, 111
Warsaw Ghetto Uprising, 75
"the West," 169–70; "the West and the Rest," global conception of, 10–11; "the West" as historical fiction, deconstruction of, 135–36
West as subject, the World as object, 7–8

Western civilization: claims, rejection of, 171; as organizing principle, end of, 155–57
Western Islamophobia, 145
Western liberalism, 82–83
Western philosophy, 82–83, 170; dehumanization logic of, 82; as historical artifact, 83–84; philosophical speculations, 85. *See also* European philosophy
Western supremacy, philosophical genealogy of, 48–49
Wolfe, Patrick, xxiii, 37, 38
Wolin, Richard, 86; *The Politics of Being*, 86
Women Without Men (film), 18
The Wretched of the Earth (Fanon), 74, 92

Yad Vashem, 33

Zionism, xxvi, 5, 10, 12, 29, 36, 141–42, 155–57, 161; as convergence of colonialism and antisemitism, 33–34; counter-Zionism, 56–57, 158–61, 164–65; Evangelical, 5, 51, 52; genocidal, xvii, 14, 84, 134, 168; history, 33, 37; 53–56; Naomi Klein on, 57–58; and liberation of Jews, Ilan Pappé on, 38–39; as part of imperial projects, 5; and settler colonialism, 37

Zuaiter, Wael, 146

ABOUT HAYMARKET BOOKS

Haymarket Books is a radical, independent, nonprofit book publisher based in Chicago. Our mission is to publish books that contribute to struggles for social and economic justice. We strive to make our books a vibrant and organic part of social movements and the education and development of a critical, engaged, and internationalist left.

We take inspiration and courage from our namesakes, the Haymarket Martyrs, who gave their lives fighting for a better world. Their 1886 struggle for the eight-hour day—which gave us May Day, the international workers' holiday—reminds workers around the world that ordinary people can organize and struggle for their own liberation. These struggles—against oppression, exploitation, environmental devastation, and war—continue today across the globe.

Since our founding in 2001, Haymarket has published more than nine hundred titles. Radically independent, we seek to drive a wedge into the risk-averse world of corporate book publishing. Our authors include Angela Y. Davis, Arundhati Roy, Keeanga-Yamahtta Taylor, Eve Ewing, Aja Monet, Mariame Kaba, Naomi Klein, Rebecca Solnit, Mohammed El-Kurd, José Olivarez, Noam Chomsky, Winona LaDuke, and Amy Goodman, among many other leading writers of our time. We are also the trade publishers of the acclaimed Historical Materialism Book Series.

Haymarket also manages a vibrant community organizing and event space in Chicago, Haymarket House, the popular Haymarket Books Live event series and podcast, and the annual Socialism Conference.

ALSO AVAILABLE FROM HAYMARKET BOOKS

By Hamid Dabashi:

Iran in Revolt
Revolutionary Aspirations in a Post-Democratic World

On Edward Said
Remembrance of Things Past

As well as:

Palestine in a World on Fire
Edited by Katherine Natanel and Ilan Pappé

Perfect Victims—And the Politics of Appeal
Mohammed El-Kurd

Their Borders, Our World
Building New Solidarities with Palestine
Edited by Mahdi Sabbagh

Visualizing Palestine
A Chronicle of Colonialism and the Struggle for Liberation
Edited by Jessica Anderson, Aline Batarseh, and
Yosra El Gazzar; created by Visualizing Palestine

ABOUT THE AUTHOR

Hamid Dabashi is the Hagop Kevorkian Professor of Iranian Studies and Comparative Literature at Columbia University. Dabashi has written more than two dozen books, edited four, and contributed chapters to many more. Among his most recent books are *On Edward Said: Remembrance of Things Past* (Haymarket Books, 2020), *The End of Two Illusions: Islam After the West* (University of California Press, 2022), and *Iran in Revolt: Revolutionary Aspirations in a Post-Democratic World* (Haymarket Books, 2025). His books and articles have been translated into numerous languages, including Japanese, German, French, Spanish, Russian, Hebrew, Arabic, and Persian.

www.ingramcontent.com/pod-product-compliance
Ingram Content Group UK Ltd.
Pitfield, Milton Keynes, MK11 3LW, UK
UKHW022033100825
461745UK00013B/357